Cambridge Elements

Elements in Eighteenth-Century Connections
edited by
Eve Tavor Bannet
University of Oklahoma
Markman Ellis
Queen Mary University of London

UNVEILING LADY SCOTT

Walter Scott, French Influence and Transcultural Connections

Céline Sabiron
University of Lorraine

Shaftesbury Road, Cambridge CB2 8EA, United Kingdom

One Liberty Plaza, 20th Floor, New York, NY 10006, USA

477 Williamstown Road, Port Melbourne, VIC 3207, Australia

314–321, 3rd Floor, Plot 3, Splendor Forum, Jasola District Centre, New Delhi – 110025, India

103 Penang Road, #05–06/07, Visioncrest Commercial, Singapore 238467

Cambridge University Press is part of Cambridge University Press & Assessment, a department of the University of Cambridge.

We share the University's mission to contribute to society through the pursuit of education, learning and research at the highest international levels of excellence.

www.cambridge.org
Information on this title: www.cambridge.org/9781009535311

DOI: 10.1017/9781009535328

© Céline Sabiron 2025

This publication is in copyright. Subject to statutory exception and to the provisions of relevant collective licensing agreements, no reproduction of any part may take place without the written permission of Cambridge University Press & Assessment.

When citing this work, please include a reference to the DOI 10.1017/9781009535328

First published 2025

A catalogue record for this publication is available from the British Library

ISBN 978-1-009-53531-1 Hardback
ISBN 978-1-009-53533-5 Paperback
ISSN 2632-5578 (online)
ISSN 2632-556X (print)

Cambridge University Press & Assessment has no responsibility for the persistence or accuracy of URLs for external or third-party internet websites referred to in this publication and does not guarantee that any content on such websites is, or will remain, accurate or appropriate.

For EU product safety concerns, contact us at Calle de José Abascal, 56, 1°, 28003 Madrid, Spain, or email eugpsr@cambridge.org

Unveiling Lady Scott

Walter Scott, French Influence and Transcultural Connections

Elements in Eighteenth-Century Connections

DOI: 10.1017/9781009535328
First published online: October 2025

Céline Sabiron
University of Lorraine
Author for correspondence: Céline Sabiron, celine.sabiron@univ-lorraine.fr

> **Abstract:** This Element sheds new light on Walter Scott's work by investigating the French influence of his wife, Charlotte Charpentier, later Lady Scott, through her transcultural upbringing and international connections. Much of the limited information about her is tainted by misconceptions from predominantly British male biographers of Scott, whose perspectives were centred on the great man and sometimes coloured by anti-French sentiment during the Revolutionary period. Drawing on new French and British public records, historical archives, annual registers, and personal materials like letters and diaries from the Scott family and their social circle, this Element dispels false allegations and reveals her significant, yet largely unacknowledged social and literary influence on Scott's writing. By analysing these sources and conducting in-depth readings of Scott's texts, the Element emphasises Scott's collaborative literary approach, arguing that Lady Scott, a knowledgeable art and literature enthusiast, greatly assisted him in his work as his secretary, amanuensis, and proofreader.

Keywords: Walter Scott, Lady Scott, transcultural connections, literary assistance, Scottish literature, French influence, transnational mediations

© Céline Sabiron 2025

ISBNs: 9781009535311 (HB), 9781009535335 (PB), 9781009535328 (OC)
ISSNs: 2632-5578 (online), 2632-556X (print)

Contents

Introduction   1

1 Veiling Lady Scott: Critical Mystification across the Channel   5

2 Mingling with a Fading Transnational Network: French Charlotte among Foreigners in Lyon   14

3 Unbecoming French: Charlotte's Shifting Identity in Cosmopolitan London   26

4 Transcultural Charlotte: Walter Scott's Creative Supporter and Literary Assistant   40

Conclusion   72

Bibliography   76

Introduction

> Who was Lady Scott originally? I really wish anybody would tell me, for surely somebody must know. There is a veil of mystery hung over that dear lady's birth and parentage, which I have been unable to see through or lift up; and there have been more lies told to me about it, and even published in all the papers of Britain, by those who *ought* to have known than ever was told about those of any woman that ever was born.[1]

Such is the question raised by the Ettrick Shepherd, as Scottish farmer and writer James Hogg was nicknamed. Lady Scott's origin and lineage reportedly stem from a mystery that not even one of Walter Scott's lifelong friends and protégés could unveil.

Acknowledging his limited knowledge of his wife's background, Scott himself displayed little curiosity about it at first. However, in a letter to his future wife dated 6 or 7 October 1797, he expressed discomfort at not being able to answer his uncle's questions about her family.[2] His initial request went unanswered, indicating that the subject might be sensitive or upsetting. Above all, it revealed her playful and high-spirited character: she was wittingly withholding information as part of a love banter reminiscient of a Marivaux comedy. The rebuffed lover, genuinely hurt, reiterated his demand on 18 October.[3] On 22 October, she responded briefly and coolly, pretending to be angry and still delaying her response. It was only three days later that she finally provided some account of her parentage.[4] This early anecdote in their relationship shows that Lady Scott herself played a role in maintaining the veil of secrecy.

In truth, aside from the handful of letters she sent to her husband-to-be, her brother, Charles, in India, her Irish guardian, Arthur Hill, later Second Marquess of Downshire, and her children's governess, Miss Millar, there are scant genuine primary sources from Lady Scott.[5] Writing was her husband's business, not hers. In a letter to their friend, playwright Joanna Baillie, on 10 June 1810, Scott aptly described his wife's growing reticence to write letters, admitting: 'She feels or rather thinks she feels difficulty in expressing herself on paper so accurately as she would. She sometimes takes fits of apprehension of this kind though she understands English like a native.'[6] Scott increasingly managed Lady Scott's responses within their social circle, including her own. Therefore, our contemporary

---

[1] Hogg, 1834: 179–180; emphasis original.
[2] Grierson, 1932–1937: I:70–71.
[3] Grierson, 1938: 56.
[4] Sept.–Dec. 1797 correspondence in 'Letters chiefly of Sir Walter Scott, 1792–1817'.
[5] The Millgate Union Catalogue of Walter Scott Correspondence lists fourteen letters written by the future Lady Scott in 1797. Additionally, the National Library of Scotland houses fifty-one letters from Scott to his wife, dated 1797, 1807, 1814, 1815, 1820, and 1821. Most of Lady Scott's letters were likely destroyed at her own request.
[6] Douglas, 1894: 1:182.

understanding of her primarily comes from her husband's diary entries and family letters and the perspectives of people who met her, as well as the imaginative narratives of those who projected their own ideals and prejudices onto her image. As the late Abbotsford archivist Kirsty Archer-Thompson brilliantly put it in her unpublished 2018 conference paper at Sorbonne University:

> It turns out, that if you look at the Letters again, she was there all along. We see her careening around in the tiny phaeton or open carriage like Titania; anxiously sending seeds and plants to friends and patrons; lovingly planting acorns with her husband; crying out in fear during thunderstorms; reclining on a sofa as James Hogg grows steadily more inebriated at her feet; making tablecloths, trout and cabbage nets by the fireside with her husband; delighting in chintz furnishings that entirely escape her husband's notice; mocking Scott's obsession with antique pistols and ugly tankards ... the list goes on. This is her fossil record. If you look again at the Letters in their entirety, Lady Scott sometimes emerges as a startingly physical presence – looking over her husband's shoulder with the same intensity she radiates from her portrait in the Abbotsford Drawing Room.[7]

Unveiling Lady Scott's French roots and transcultural connections, and assessing her influence on her husband's writing, requires us to read between the lines and look askance, as if through anamorphosis. Besides, it demands unbiased judgement and thorough cross-checking of statements, given that the veil around her has only thickened due to the intense emotional involvement across the Channel over the past two centuries.

Rather than focusing solely on her French lineage and individual identity, a more insightful approach, I argue, is to explore her evolution into a transnational and transcultural figure by considering the significant Franco-British interactions that occurred during the late eighteenth century. In order to dispel misconceptions surrounding her, this Element includes insights into Lyon and its British community prior to the French Revolution. It draws on primary sources such as the Lyon almanacs of 1743 and 1772, as well as seminal critical works by Pierre Grosclaude and Louis Trénard. Unpublished details about the Lyon Royal Academy of Equitation, where Lady Scott was raised, are taken from a 1771 document held in the 'Rare and Special Books' collection at the Lyon Municipal Library. It was written by her father, Jean Charpentier, who was the academy's head at the time. Further insights are from Charles Duplessis' (1892) detailed work on equitation in France.

---

[7] Archer-Thompson, 2018. As this conference paper remains unpublished, no page number is available for this reference. I am deeply grateful to Kirsty Archer-Thompson for generously sharing it with me just a few months before her death, and I hope to honour her insights by including her findings in this Element.

The second shortcoming in earlier studies of Lady Scott stems from the investigators' background. Predominantly British and male, their focus was primarily on Scott and his work. They showed minimal interest in his wife and had limited access to French resources. Chronicling his visit to Abbotsford in 1817, Washington Irving concluded his Scott-focused narrative by saying: 'I took a kind farewell of the [Scott] family, with each of whom I had been highly pleased; if I have refrained from dwelling particularly on their several characters, and giving anecdotes of them individually, it is because I consider them shielded by the sanctity of domestic life: Scott, on the contrary, belongs to history.'[8] Irving's statement uncovers a glaring truth: in most Scott biographies until the 1970s – marking the development of women's studies and contributions of female biographers like Dame Una Pope-Hennessy, Carola Oman, and Eileen Dunlop – with the exception of Hesketh Pearson's (1954) biography, Lady Scott was relegated to the sidelines, viewed as merely anecdotal, a minor character lost in the family's collective dynamic. Confined to the domestic sphere and the realm of the intimate, she was made invisible and thus in essence erased from existence, at least as far as substantial literary records are concerned. Living in 'Scott's Shadow', to quote Ian Duncan, she was excluded from history, a domain reserved for her husband, the master of historical fiction. Dispossessed of her heritage, she was also stripped of any historical legacy.

As she entered the realm of romance and fiction, there has been an almost irresistible temptation to engage in over-interpretation regarding narratives about her. Adapting Isabelle Bour's phrase, I believe that in Lady Scott's case there is an implicit 'injunction to emplotment' – that is, a prevalent, concerted effort, often by male commentators assuming narrative authority, to assign her life a specific storyline.[9] This narrative authority starts with her name, a blend of borrowed and fabricated elements. Known as 'Lady Scott' after marrying the famed father of the historical novel in 1797, she carried the title 'Lady', not as a consequence of her own social rank, but as the wife of a baronet – a title bestowed upon the Scott family on 22 April 1820. This title indicates her status as the spouse of a baronet, not a baronetess in her own right. This naming effectively reduces her identity to a borrowed surname and a granted title, overshadowing her true origins and life story. As a result, a fictionalised narrative about her life was perpetuated in newspapers and her husband's biographies, transforming her into a fictionalised subject. This mystification

---

[8] Irving, 1835: 264.
[9] Discussing Lockhart's narrative mode, which favours 'showing' over 'telling', Bour talked about a 'refusal of emplotment', Bour, 1996: 39.

was exacerbated by the scarcity of details regarding her life and the seamless appearance of Scott's own life.[10]

Adopting a transnational perspective that encompasses her distinct profile within the broader context of migration between France and Britain, and transcending the prevalent anti-French biases of the early nineteenth century – impoverished yet cultured French émigrés, endowed with refined manners, were typically welcomed in Britain in the initial stages – this study aims to integrate Lady Scott into literary history, not merely as an intriguing spouse, but as a pivotal figure who shaped Scott's world view and influenced his literary oeuvre.[11] Taking a historico-biographical and revisionist approach in this Element, I believe that to fully grasp Walter Scott's writings, one must go a step further and recognise the potential for his texts to engage in a dialogue with their author and his life. Following feminist scholars like Simone de Beauvoir in *The Second Sex* (1949), Elaine Showalter in *A Literature of Their Own* (1977), and Sandra Gilbert and Susan Gubar in *The Madwoman in the Attic* (1979), I position myself within an inclusive history that embraces women and other marginalised groups historically excluded from dominant narratives.

Moreover, this Element contributes to current research in literary studies on 'social authorship' and collaborative practices, further challenging the perception of Scott as the solitary 'Wizard of the North'.[12] It posits that the extensive corpus of his work was the result of a collaborative endeavour, with significant contributions from women, notably through Lady Scott's role within Scott's female literary circle. This perspective builds on the idea of collaborative production, as suggested by Ina Ferris (2012) in 'Scott's Authorship and Book Culture'. It also expands upon the concept of a 'multi-handed' writing technique, a theme I explored in my article published in the 2017 Modern Humanities Research Association 'Yearbook of English Studies' dedicated to Walter Scott.

This Element is divided into four sections tracing Lady Scott's chronological journey across geographical, national, and identity boundaries. It follows her transition from a fading transnational network in Lyon, to her unbecoming French in London, and finally to her embracing a transcultural identity within Scott's literary circle. From now on, I will refer to Lady Scott as Charlotte

---

[10] 'Scott's everyday life was anything but romantic or romance-like, rigorously divided as it was into periods devoted to well-defined activities. There was no plot in that life, only a repeated pattern with variations,' Bour, 1996: 40.

[11] The French were initially popular as a novelty, especially before 1793 when Britain joined the war against France. However, after years of appeals for support and as the war dragged on, the British grew increasingly weary of their presence.

[12] See Oman's (1973) biography of Scott, *The Wizard of the North*, whose title was inspired by the nickname given to John Henry Anderson (1814–1874), seen as the first Scottish magician.

Charpentier – and as Charlotte Scott in Section 4 – even though it differs from her birth name, as will be explained in Section 3. However, I prefer using the name Charlotte Charpentier, which not only reflects her commonly used name, but also underscores her French origin and transcultural journey, giving her a full and singular identity separate from that of her husband.[13]

1 Veiling Lady Scott: Critical Mystification across the Channel

The playful yet tense epistolary correspondence between Scott and his future wife about her lineage in 1797 foreshadowed the media battle that would unfold in Britain and France over the next two centuries. This section takes the form of a literature review with a comparative approach, exploring Charlotte's varying fortunes in the two countries, where she was generally portrayed more favorably in France than in Britain. It traces shifting trends over three distinct periods marked by major publications or Scott's anniversaries: before 1837, between 1837 and 1932, and from the 1970s and 1980s onward.

The first hints of some confusion about her parentage appeared in the 'Miscellaneous' section of the *Manchester Courier* published a couple of months after Scott's death on 17 November 1832:

> The Late Lady Scott. – There appears to be a considerable difference of opinion respecting the maiden name of the wife of the late Sir Walter Scott. For instance, the *John Bull* says Sir Walter Scott married a lady, Miss Charpentier, daughter of a Swiss emigrant; 'Miss Carpenter, daughter of a gentleman of Jersey', says Allan Cunningham; Miss Carpentier, daughter of a merchant at Lyons, according to Chambers; and Miss Charpentier, a French emigré, if we believe the *Atlas*.[14]

From 1832 to 1837 quite a few journalistic sketches and book-length lives of Scott were produced in Britain, some by the writer's closest friends. Each offered diverging and often disparaging information about Charlotte, as Hogg encapsulated in the quote used as this Element's epigraph. The one exception was John Gibson Lockhart's monumental seven-volume biography, which marked a turning point in 1837. It became the definitive official account of Scott's life for the next century, overshadowing earlier and contemporary portraits despite the underlying criticism of its panegyric tone.

---

[13] 'Il semble bien qu'en dépit de l'acte de baptême, le prénom de Charlotte fut habituellement donné à Marguerite Charpentier, peut-être en souvenir de sa mère,' Martin-Basse, 1932: 2.

[14] 'The Late Lady Scott', 1832: 4. The given references are the satirical *John Bull* Sunday newspaper, Allan Cunningham's *Some Account of the Life and Works of Sir Walter Scott* (1832), Robert Chambers' *Life of Sir Walter Scott* (1832), and an article from the *Atlas* (Sunday, 11 Nov. 1832: 8).

1.1 Charlotte in the Shadows: Diverging Portraits in Britain and France

The legitimacy of Lockhart's *Memoirs of the Life of Sir Walter Scott* (1837–1838) – and its corollary downside as he was accused of nepotism and portraying the Scotts too favourably – stemmed from his position as Scott's son-in-law and, together with his wife, Scott's eldest daughter, Sophia, as guardian of Scott's literary legacy.[15] Additionally, the biography's key strengths lay in its 'prevalence of documentary material over authorial/authoritative telling' and its 'careful avoidance of narrative guidance', along with its apparent ability to resolve discrepancies, thereby seemingly lifting the veil of mystery surrounding Charlotte Charpentier's orgins.[16]

Excerpts about Charlotte were thus widely shared and quoted, not only in British national[17] and regional newspapers, but also in French publications like *Revue britannique*.[18] This magazine, renowned for sharing articles from leading British periodicals, featured numerous extracts from Lockhart's biography, probably translated by Amédée Pichot – a critic and translator of Scott's works who became the magazine's chief editor in 1739. Other translated extracts appeared as articles in *Le Constitutionnel*[19] or as a serial in *Journal de Paris* under 'Correspondance littéraire de Walter Scott', which included transcribed letters between Scott and his wife-to-be.[20]

It must be said that Scott was immensely popular in France at the time. As a Scottish author, he benefitted from France's long-standing relationship with Scotland, which dated back to the Auld Alliance (1295) against England in the Middle Ages. This connection continued unbroken into the eighteenth century, through the Age of Enlightenment,[21] and thrived long after the 1707 Acts of Union and the Entente Cordiale of 1904, according to British historian Siobhan Talbott.[22] Despite a slowdown in literary exchanges and trade between France and England during the Revolution and the Napoleonic Wars, Scotland was

---

[15] 'That Lockhart, with his close family ties, censored materials, seems beyond any doubt. His treatment of all members of the Scott household is as reverential as one would expect from a son and sibling-in-law,' Archer-Thompson, 2018.
[16] Bour, 1996: 38–39.
[17] There were articles in *The Globe*, *Atlas*, *The Morning Gazette*, *The Morning Chronicle*, *The Morning Post* etc.
[18] Reprints of Lockhart's biography of Scott were accessible in English in Paris. These editions were issued by the Galignani brothers and their main rival, Louis-Claude Baudry, who also specialised in publishing works written in foreign languages.
[19] 'Walter Scott: son enfance et sa jeunesse racontée par lui-même' (1837) and 'Mémoires sur la vie de Walter Scott, par J. G. Lockhart' (1838).
[20] 'Feuilleton: Conseils de Walter Scott à son fils' (1837); 'Feuilleton: Correspondance littéraire de Walter Scott' (1837). *Journal de Paris* was the first daily newspaper in France and it was modelled after *The London Evening Post*.
[21] Broadie, 2012. [22] Talbott, 2014.

mostly unaffected. French and Scottish works thus circulated abundantly across the Channel, with Scottish philosophy influencing French painting, and James Macpherson's *Ossian* shaping the development of French Romanticism. Key ideas impacted areas such as children's moral education and the relationship between reflection and perception in the arts and moral life. These topics are explored by Deidre Dawson and Pierre Morère (2004) in their *Scotland and France in the Enlightenment*. Scottish philosophers like David Hume, Adam Smith, and Adam Ferguson were introduced to French readers in translation relatively late, during the first half of the nineteenth century. However, this late Scottish craze in France was quite beneficial as it also included more literary figures such as Macpherson, Robert Burns, and Scott, who reached the height of his fame starting in 1809 with the publication of *Marmion*.[23]

Scott even became a staple in French media, with his presence dramatically escalating from 1819 – from 14 articles to a striking 665 by 1832.[24] He was so popular in France that the term 'Scottophilia' aptly described the French reception of his work.[25] This admiration was sparked by early translations of his works, such as Joseph Martin's 1816 French rendition of *Guy Mannering* and the 1817 translations of *The Antiquary* by Sophie de Maraise and Auguste Jean-Baptiste Defauconpret. Despite their imperfections,[26] Defauconpret's translations were pivotal in popularising Scott's works, notably with *Les Puritains d'Écosse*.[27] 'Over the course of the nineteenth century, they [Scott's novels] became an integral part of French literature,' especially after Scott's second visit to Paris in 1826.[28] His celebrity status was unmistakable: he was warmly received and showered with compliments and gifts, indicating the depth of his influence and popularity: '1822–7 seem from the publishing history to have been the main years of Scott fever in France'.[29] He was so much appropriated by the French that 'this was the time when the French press only talked about the Great Scotsman' and his literary work, with only occasional mentions of his wife.[30]

---

[23] *Gazette de France*, 1809; *Gazette nationale ou le Moniteur universel* 1810 and 1811; *Journal de l'Empire*, 1812 and 1813; *Gazette Nationale ou le Moniteur universel*, 1813; *Journal de Paris*, 1813; *Mercure de France*, 1813; *Journal des arts et de la politique*, 1815; *Journal Général de France*, 1816; *La Quotidienne*, 1816.

[24] There were 14 articles in 1819, 52 in 1820, 69 in 1821, 75 in 1822, 91 in 1823, 155 in 1824, 233 in 1825, and 370 in 1826 but none on Lady Scott's death, 341 in 1827 because of the *Life of Napoleon Buonaparte*, 298 in 1828, 390 in 1829, and 665 in 1832, the year of his death.

[25] Maxwell, 2009: 251; 'Scott in France' in Pittock, 2006: 6.

[26] 'Le succès de Scott devient foudroyant vers 1820, malgré la fadeur et l'inexactitude des traductions de Defauconpret et ses confrères,' Bernard, 1996: 48.

[27] 'Defauconpret's *Les Puritains d'Ecosse* [*Old Mortality*] gave Scott his first French success and first major European breakthrough,' Barnaby, 2006: 34.

[28] Maxwell, 2006: 12.   [29] Lyons, 1984: 27.   [30] My translation, Maigron, 1912: 52.

Because the nineteenth-century French media drew inspiration from and modelled themselves after leading British newspapers such as the highly influential *Edinburgh Review*, launched in Scotland in 1802, and the *Quarterly Review* in London in 1809, they closely followed and directly translated British sources. There was an immediate and seamless transfer of information across the Channel. As a result, both British and French publications either romanticised Charlotte's chance encounter with Scott in Cumberland at the fashionable Gilsland spa resort, or shared gossip about her origins.[31] For example, the 3 December 1837 edition of *Journal de Paris* reported on the rumours of her illegitimacy as mentioned in George Allan's (1834) biography of Scott.[32] It was speculated that her alleged benefactor, Arthur Hill, the Marquess of Downshire, was actually her father, and that the woman acting as her chaperone, Jane Nicolson, was in reality her mother. Even though these allegations freely crossed borders, aside from similar questions about her origins, her image in France remained much more positive. She was portrayed as a devoted wife and mother, blessing her Scottish husband with sons and daughters. Scott was seen as fortunate, having made a beneficial marriage due to her dowry – converted into francs and sometimes inflated.[33] Often 'Frenchified', she was consistently referred to as Charlotte Charpentier, with the title of Lady Scott typically reserved for the wife of their eldest son.

Conversely, in Britain, the lack of authentic information about Charlotte – combined with a potential lingering anti-French sentiment among some later critics and commentators – led to a widespread trend of circulating hearsay or reporting derogatory comments about her 'broken English'[34] or lack of 'depth and intensity'.[35] The prevailing negativity in Britain rendered Lockhart's reverential treatment of the Scott household a particularly conspicuous exception, dividing critics and serving to intensify opposing views about her. His second 1839 edition, which included minor corrections and some additions before being more fully revised in 1848, couldn't entirely quell accusations of

---

[31] During the 1871 centenary of Scott's birth, French and English headlines about her often read like 'Sir Walter Scott's Courtship'(*Bolton Free Press*, 1837: 4), 'Sir Walter Scott's First and Second Love' (*Liverpool Albion*, 1837: 7), or 'Sir Walter Scott's Connection with Cumberland' (*Carlisle Patriot*, 1871: 4). 'Mr Walter Scott se rend à cheval à Gilsland, petite ville d'eau du Cumberland. Il croise, à son arrivée, une jeune fille, également montée, qui, à première vue, charme ses regards. Le même soir, il la retrouve à un bal, et lui est présenté: Lieutenant Scott, d'Édimbourg; Miss Charlotte Carpenter, de Carlisle. Ils dansèrent, et se plurent,' 'Walter Scott et la France ... de son temps', Roth, 1932: 191.

[32] Allan, 1834: 183–184 cited in translation in *Journal de Paris*, 1837: 1.

[33] 'Melle Marguerite-Charlotte Charpentier, une Lyonnaise calviniste, que la Révolution avait chassée de France et qui devait donner au jeune avocat deux fils et autant de filles. Walter Scott venait de faire ce qu'on est convenu d'appeler une union avantageuse: Melle Charpentier lui rapportait bien 10 000 francs de rente,' Descours, 1895: 4.

[34] Hutton, 1878: 34–35.   [35] Lang, 1906: 26.

emotional bias. 'There are mysteries about Charlotte's background and about her mother's relationship with Lord Downshire; Lockhart's account of Mme Charpentier as a French Royalist fleeing the Revolution with her children is now known to be an invention,' David Daiches (1971) concluded in his book *Sir Walter Scott and His World*.[36] From the 1830s to the 1930s, the veil over Lady Scott was further obscured by a lack of critical distance, shaped primarily by national preferences – patriotism in France and some anti-French sentiment later in Britain – as well as emotional partiality in Lockhart's biography, driven by personal vested interests.

1.2 Charlotte in the Spotlight: The 1930s Press Battle and Unveiling Advances

The 1932 anniversary of Scott's death sparked a surge in publications about her husband, but he was not the sole subject of attention. For the first time, Charlotte also became a focus of articles, to the point that unveiling her true origins ignited a heated debate following the publication of Scottish barrister and journalist Donald Carswell's (1930) *Sir Walter: A Four-Part Study in Biography*. Over the next six months, no fewer than nine letters and articles – framed as prosecutions or defenses – appeared in *The Scotsman*, turning it into a sort of media courtroom. Key contributors like Scottish minister Dr William Shillinglaw Crockett (1930b) and Professor Herbert J. C. Grierson (1930) successively stepped forward to challenge Carswell's methods and conclusions.

The significant benefit of all this media uproar was to bring Charlotte out of her husband's shadow and into the spotlight, triggering research on her rather than solely on Scott. Wilfred Partington (1932) contributed to this shift by introducing new documents from Scott's unpublished letter books in his *Sir Walter's Post-Bag*, including a letter from Charlotte's guardian, Arthur Hill.[37] Taking this further, Grierson's (1938) *Sir Walter Scott, Bart.: A New Life* – intended as a 'supplement' and correction to Lockhart's biography – conducted thorough research into Charlotte's background, unearthing key documents like a letter from French Abbé de Chazelle about Charlotte's mother, and included lengthy chapters on 'Charlotte at Gilsland' and 'Charlotte, her brother and Miss Nicolson'.[38] Grierson was soon invited across the Channel to

---

[36] Daiches, 1971: 55. See also 'This was extraordinarily full of errors,' Oman, 1973: 360.
[37] Partington, 1932: 4–5.
[38] '*The Life of Sir Walter Scott* has been written by Lockhart in a manner that is not likely to be superseded or rivalled. But Lockhart's is a carefully composed picture in which some features of the original have been omitted, others skillfully softened; and the many letters which are now available show not only much inaccuracy in the details of Lockhart's narrative but a somewhat surprising element of what appears to be sheer invention of a picturesque and dramatic

deliver a lecture at the Sorbonne University on 22 April 1932, as advertised by *Comoedia* in the newspaper's 'Voici Paris' section (p. 5).

As a result, in France, numerous newspapers commemorated Scott,[39] with a few dedicating significant space to his wife, like *Excelsior* featuring a full article in its 'Le Monde' column on 1 October 1932.[40] These pieces continued to highlight her French origins – a point of national pride – and to portray her in a charming, naive, and romanticised manner as a French refugee from the Revolution. However, for the first time, they hinted at her contribution to Scott's novelistic destiny. Martin-Basse's article 'La femme de Walter Scott' (Figure 1), published in *Journal des débats politiques et littéraires* (21 sept. 1932), came with a description of an 1817 family painting by David Wilkie, published in an 1895 issue of *Les Contemporains* (Figure 2).[41]

The image (Figure 2) was meant to convey domestic happiness, bucolic simplicity, and pastoral bliss, while also emphasising the central role of family for Scott, particularly his wife, in a vivid and emotionally charged caption: 'dressed as a farmer's wife, a basket on her arm, here smiles the mother of the family, Marguerite Charpentier, the woman from Lyon whom Walter Scott married and who was the joy of his life'.[42]

From then on, interest in Charlotte and her impact was sparked on both sides of the Channel and continued to grow over the years, though unevenly, as Scott's work fell out of favour between the 1930s and 1970s, dismissed as childish and outdated. However, there were two notable exceptions during this period.

In her biography of Scott, British historian Dame Pope-Hennessy (1948: 51–60) referenced Charlotte throughout, devoting nine pages to exploring autobiographical elements in Scott's work and highlighting Charlotte's influence. She built on John Buchan's (1932) work, which briefly paralleled her to Julia Mannering from *Guy Mannering* through a single, very succinct sentence with no further development ('He was afterwards to draw her portrait in Julia Mannering,' Buchan, 1932: 55). Pope-Hennessy was the first to suggest Charlotte's inspirational influence on her husband's writing.

---

character.... The aim of the present biography is, therefore, not to rival Lockhart's or other of the many Lives based on that work, but rather to supplement,' Grierson, 1938: 1.

[39] See the obituary section in *Le Figaro*, 1832: 1–2.

[40] 'Lady Scott, à qui son mari témoigna toujours un tendre attachement, était une Française. Une Lyonnaise, pour être précis: Charlotte Charpentier avant son mariage. C'était une jolie brune qui adorait les belles robes.... Elle fut toujours une hôtesse charmante pour les amis de son mari,' *Excelsior*, 'Lady Scott', 1932: 2.

[41] Descoux, 1895: 1.

[42] My translation, 'vêtue en fermière, un panier au bras, sourit la mère de famille, Marguerite Charpentier, la Lyonnaise que Walte Scott épousa et qui fut la joie de sa vie', Martin-Basse, 1932: 2.

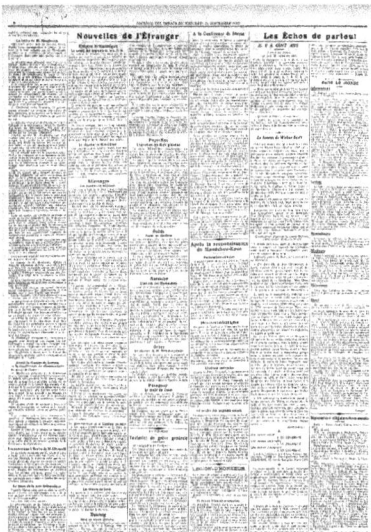

Figure 1 Martin-Basse, 'La femme de Walter Scott', credit to Bibliothèque nationale de France.

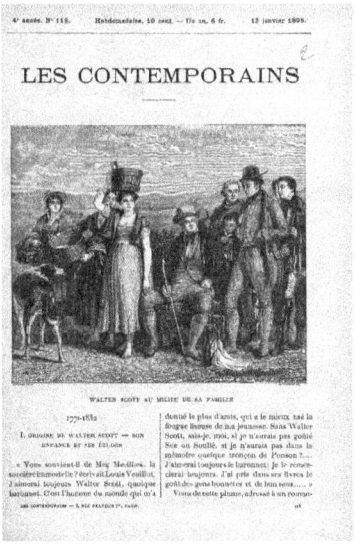

Figure 2 Descoux, 'Walter Scott', credit to Bibliothèque nationale de France.

The second exception came with Hesketh Pearson's (1954) *Walter Scott: His Life and Personality*. Pearson, a popular biographer, dedicated five pages to Charlotte, sharing anecdotes that vividly portrayed her and, for the first time, gave her a voice through the medium of humorous quotes. Lady Scott's 'physical presence', previously noted by Archer-Thompson, became increasingly tangible. Both Pope-Hennessy's and Pearson's portrayals brought her to life, giving her depth and substance in a way that had not been achieved before.

1.3 Charlotte in an Inclusive History

The last major turning point in research on Charlotte Charpentier came in the 1970s and 1980s, marked by a surge of publications on Scott – twelve biographies[43] and two major critical studies – coinciding with the bicentenary of his birth.[44] The change in perspective on Charlotte initiated by Pope-Hennessy and Pearson was progressively solidified in the next two biographies of Scott reflecting the rise of women's studies. Featuring at length, though still relegated to the appendix in Carola Oman's (1973) biography ('Who was Lady Scott?'), Charlotte moved further from being a marginal note in the paratext to a central figure in Eileen Dunlop's (2016) biography of Scott.[45] Dunlop's four-page chapter compassionately dedicated to 'Charlotte' was symbolically placed in the main body and at the heart of her book.[46] Though neither of these books introduced new material on Charlotte – they mostly pointed to the veil of mystery surrounding her (Dunlop, 2016: 83) and discussed the various versions of her story – they had the merit of giving her a more prominent place in her husband's biography than ever before. It is likely no coincidence that they were written by female authors attuned to 'this new era of "herstory"'.[47]

And yet, another work – a typescript left unpublished and gathering dust at the National Library of Scotland since 1972 – offers extremely valuable new insights, not only into Charlotte Charpentier's origins, but also into her influence on Scott's work, based on extensive research. American independent researcher and feminist Elizabeth A. Dexter dedicated seven years (1955–1962) to researching Charlotte, with help from her friend Dr MacKay Quynn, who conducted research in French archives on her behalf. Dexter also corresponded extensively with Scott specialists, including the librarian and Scottophile James C. Corson, as well as Grierson and Pope-Hennessy, as documented in her 'Papers' stored at the Edinburgh University

---

[43] Quayle, 1968; Clark, 1969; Jeffares, 1969; MacNalty, 1969; Johnson, 1970; Daiches, 1971; Oman, 1973; Hewitt, 1981; MacMaster, 1981; Bold, 1983; Millgate, 1984; Lauber, 1989.
[44] Bell, 1973 and Alexander and Hewitt, 1983.
[45] Oman, 1973: 359–365. This appendix built upon an article written a couple of years earlier titled 'The True Scott', Oman, 1971: 36.
[46] Dunlop, 2016: 83–87.   [47] Archer-Thompson, 2018.

Library. The content of her thesis, 'Sir Walter Scott and His Wife: The Happy Marriage and the Mystery',[48] has never been explored before, except as a brief reference in Deirdre Shepherd's talk on Charlotte Charpentier at the Edinburgh Sir Walter Scott Club on 7 March 2019.[49] Why? Probably for three reasons: first, its limited availability for on-site consultation only; second, its idealised tone, which offers a highly factual sensationalist narrative typical of popular American biographies but often lacks depth and critical distance; and third, its incomplete citations, which require extensive fact-checking to be usable. And yet Dexter's work, exclusively centred on Charlotte Charpentier, does reveal new documents and previously unpublished valuable information that deserve to be used and shared for the first time in this Element, following thorough cross-checking of facts and archives.

In France, it wasn't until the 1990s that French academic Henri Suhamy (1993) authored the acclaimed biography *Walter Scott: Inventeur du roman historique*, aiming to revive the legacy of the overlooked Scottish writer.[50] Suhamy dedicated a whole section to 'gay and elegant'[51] Charlotte Charpentier, noting the mysteries of her past,[52] but only to conclude: 'these family mysteries are of no real importance'.[53]

In line with Suhamy's approach, my objective is not to lift the 'veil of mystery' around Lady Scott. This veil is likely too dense – due to a lack of primary and reliable secondary sources – and has been further embroidered by numerous commentators, making definitive removal challenging, to say the least. Over the years, many scholars, as demonstrated in this section, have struggled with the task. The veil is perhaps paradoxically both unremovable and inevitable as a necessary evil and a sign of the 'Spirit of the Age'. History was public and most women were absent from the public sphere. They were confined to the domestic and private sphere. It was also an era marked by romanticised narratives that blurred fiction and reality and harboured prejudices against Revolutionary France, particularly viewing French women as immoral degenerates.

As evidenced by this historical media and biographical analysis, the inquiry about Scott's wife was flawed from the outset. The flaw lay in the nature of the question, that of her origins, which oversimplified her inherently complex and multifaceted character shaped by her family's varying fortunes and the pivotal era she lived in. Our goal here is to reframe her transcultural story within the

---

[48] https://manuscripts.nls.uk/repositories/2/resources/19888.
[49] 'The Life of Marguerite Charlotte Charpentier: Disorderly Other' for 'The Edinburgh Sir Walter Scott Club', 7 March 2019. www.youtube.com/watch?v=2rA8DfZYiTo.
[50] Henri Suhamy published another booklet on Walter Scott in 2022, but there were few allusions to Charlotte. Suhamy, 2022: 15–16.
[51] Suhamy, 1993: 85–89.   [52] Suhamy, 1993: 91.   [53] My translation, Suhamy, 1993: 87.

context of Franco-British history and the long-standing relationship between the two countries, particularly with Scotland.

2 Mingling with a Fading Transnational Network: French Charlotte among Foreigners in Lyon

Charlotte Charpentier was raised in a cosmopolitan, transnational bourgeois society during a critical time, both personally and historically. Her father's recent promotion to the king's equerry, placing him at the head of the Royal Academy of Equitation, an elite international school based in Lyon, coincided with the institution's inevitable decline, leading to its closure in 1789. Charlotte's formative years in France were thus marked by stark contrasts and upheavals as she experienced the dramatic rise and fall of her family's status, all against the backdrop of the French Revolution.

2.1 The Well-Connected Charpentier Household and the Lyon Royal Academy of Equitation

As demonstrated in Section 1, tracing Charlotte Charpentier's origin in Lyon is very challenging, even for a French critic, because very few archives survive from that period. Either no records were kept, or they were lost or destroyed during the French Revolution, as was the case with most documents, including the lists of teachers and students from the Lyon Royal Academy of Equitation. Reconstructing Charlotte's background requires cross-referencing various sources such as archives, almanacs, and historians' accounts, including the work of Charles Duplessis and Corinne Doucet on academies and horse riding in France.

It also requires some understanding of historical variations in French spelling, a significant challenge for anglophone critics. At the turn of the century, French – especially patronyms – was still written phonetically, even as public education and mass printing began to standardise spelling. As a result, the Charpentiers' identity was fluid, with the spelling of their names varying widely. This is evident in the inconsistent spellings of Charlotte's mother's maiden name across documents: Marguerite Charlotte Volère (1749–1788?) appeared as 'Vollaire' on her baptism register, 'Volaire' on her wedding certificate, and 'Volere' in the family Bible at Abbotsford. Manuscripts also reveal graphic variations in homophonic endings like 'è', 'ai', and 'ay', as seen in Abbé de Chazelle's letter reproduced in Section 2.3 ('Mme Volayre'). These variations stem from their shared phoneme, the [e] sound, at a time when orthographic standards were still evolving. Similarly, the family surname fluctuated, predominantly appearing as 'Charpentier', but occasionally as 'Charpentié'.[54]

---

[54] This spelling is recorded on the 1771 prospectus of the Military Academy for Gentlemen, 'run by Mr Charpentié'.

Furthermore, human error contributed to these spelling and graphic variations. For example, the first name 'Élie' was erroneously listed on the baptism register of Charlotte's mother. This mistake was corrected to 'Marguerite Charlotte Volaire' on her wedding certificate, a name then consistently used on her children's birth certificates.[55] Regarding Charlotte's father, his full name was Jean François Charpentier – with 'François' being his middle name, like 'Charlotte' for his wife – but there were inconsistencies in the sources. The fluctuation between his first (Jean) and middle (François) names has caused confusion, leading some critics to incorrectly assume his full first name was 'Jean-François'.

Alongside these historical spelling inconsistencies and human errors stemming from a lack of understanding of French naming conventions at the time, the general lack of interest in Charlotte Charpentier has made even identifying her name a source of confusion and errors. As Archer-Thompson explained:

> A brief trawl online or a flick through the pages of any modest library of Scott criticism will likely unearth a Charlotte Marguerite Charpentier alongside her ghostly doppelganger, Marguerite Charlotte, often with another name, Geneviève, floating somewhere in the ether. She is notoriously hard to pin down. Namelessness and mistaken identity seems to be part of her creed.[56]

It is all the more part of her creed, since her husband unwittingly contributed to it. Walter Scott famously indulged in identity play and anonymity game, 'staging ... fake competing auctorial identities' through a 'process of fictional self-construction'.[57] The Author of Waverley, with his 'inbuilt plurality', excelled in crafting smokescreens and diversions, skilfully leading his readers in dizzying circles.[58] His statement to his maternal aunt, Miss Christian Rutherford, in an 8 October 1797 letter, that 'She was born in France – her parents were of English extraction – the name Carpenter. She was left an orphan early in life, and educated in England,' only deepened critics' confusion.[59] Scott undoubtedly bent the truth to make his choice of bride more acceptable to his family. However, his inaccurate account of Charlotte's origins only added fuel to speculative theories about her origins. Yet, with a bit of perseverance, some background knowledge of French spelling and naming history, and extensive research, a considerable number of facts can be uncovered.

Charlotte Charpentier's parents were worldy devoted royalists. Charlotte's mother came from high ranks, 'belong[ing] to an old French house' based in

---

[55] In this Element, she will never be referred to as 'Élie' but as 'Marguerite', except in quotations where the name differs.
[56] Archer-Thompson, 2018.   [57] Sabiron, 2017: 61, 62.   [58] Ferris, 2012: 18.
[59] Scott, 1896: 182.

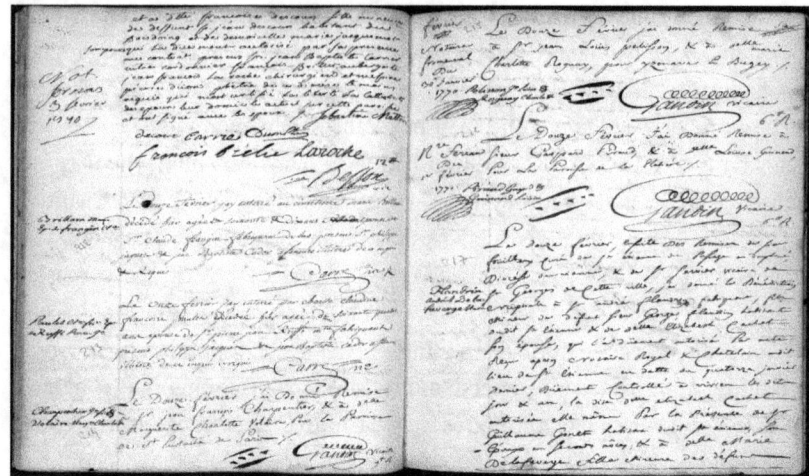

Figure 3 Marriage certificate, Lyon's Municipal Archives, credit to Ville de Lyon, Archives municipales, registre paroissial de Saint-Nizier (1770, cote 1GG 198, acte 214).

Paris.[60] Hence, in early 1770, the Charpentiers married not in Lyon but in Paris, at the St Eustache parish, as proved by the marriage certificate signed by Vicaire Gandin and stored at Lyon's Municipal Archives (Figure 3).[61]

Charlotte's father was equally cosmopolitan and had even more transcultural connections than her mother. He had served as the controller to the household of the French Embassy in Constantinople for two decades. Born in 1725, he was twenty-four years his wife's senior and had seen much of the world. He was thus well travelled and had engaged with influential French and international figures, even if his contributions – centred on financial management, logistical support, administrative oversight, procurement, and the recruitment, training, and supervision of local embassy staff – were largely behind the scenes. This explains why no evidence remains of his tenure at Constantinople where he attended ambassador Charles Gravier, comte de Vergennes, from 1755, just before the Seven Years' War: Jean Charpentier is nowhere mentioned in the diplomat's correspondence stored at the French National Archives. In 1768, he returned to France with Vergennes, who was recalled along with several of his key superintendents. After a three-year withdrawal in disgrace for marrying his mistress, widow Anne Duvivier, without seeking the king's consent – a requirement for French ambassadors – Vergennes was nevertheless appointed ambassador to Stockholm from 1771 to 1774 before ascending to the position of secretary of state for foreign affairs under Louis XVI.

---

[60] Rogers, 1877: lxiv–lxv. See also '[Mme Charpentier's] brother, Chevalier Volere, was killed in action in 1813,' Crockett, 1930a.

[61] See Archives de Lyon, cote 1GG198: 53.

This remarkable rise, facilitated by Comte de Broglie, then leading the king's secret cabinet, also benefitted his contacts, including Charpentier.

While in Constantinople, the latter had engaged with many well-connected foreigners, in particular attendees of successive British ambassadors Sir James Porter (1747–1762), Henry Grenville (1761–1765), and John Murray (1766–1775). These international connections and his service to his country and King Louis XV proved crucial when he returned to his home town, Lyon, in 1768. While abroad, he had also gathered enough money to buy out the investment of Dominique-Antoine Payr-Morello, a naturalised Italian who was then head of the Lyon Royal Academy of Equitation. After negotiating with him for some time, Jean Charpentier was eventually appointed head of the prestigious institution from 1 March 1771. This took place about a year after his marriage and a couple of months after Charlotte's birth on 16 December 1770.[62]

Influenced by and modelled after their Italian counterparts, the French Academies, such as the one in Lyon established in 1651, 'aimed at the apprenticeship, training and education of the nobility'.[63] In the almanac of the city of Lyon, the 'King's Academy for the education of young noblemen', as it is called, is described as 'one of the oldest in the Kingdom, and it has always been frequented by foreigners, when the war ceased to arm the Princes of Europe. Mathematics, military exercises, and the art of horse riding, dancing, and vaulting, etc. are taught there'.[64] On top of the standard subjects, 'a long list of elective courses was offered also, – drawings, writings, singing, instrumental music, music appreciation, law, geography, heraldry, and fables, in fact as the brochure modestly asserted, "everything necessary to cultivate individual talents"',[65] Dexter reported in her thesis. Therefore, gradually more focused on the etiquette and the fine education of the court than the military art of the war, royal academies were seen as places where noblemen, whether from France or abroad, could learn how to best serve royalty and forge crucial social connections for their future. The Lyon Academy was reputed to be one of the most highly regarded institutions in Europe according to Jean de Saint-Aubain in *Histoire de la ville de Lyon* (1666). Strategically situated in the Perrache district, near the Ainay church,[66] this establishment, alongside the veterinary school – the first of its kind in the world – played a pivotal role in establishing Lyon as a centre for intellectual growth.

The Academy enlisted quite a few foreigners, like young Welsh landowner Wyrriott Owen (1752–1780), about whom a fair amount is known due to a

---

[62] He must have met Marguerite Volère after his return, probably in 1768 – that is, a couple of years before marrying her.
[63] My translation, Doucet, 2003/2004: 817.
[64] My translation, *Almanach de la ville de Lyon*, 1772: 200.   [65] Dexter, 1960: 145.
[66] Degueurce, 2012: 337.

judicial case involving Mme Charpentier, Charlotte's mother. After going to Eton (1764–1767) and then Christ's College, Cambridge, from May 1768 to midsummer 1770,[67] Owen likely attended the Academy some time between 1773 and 1775 as evidenced by the 'Owen v. Morgan' case at the Chancery Court: '[he] did sometimes in or about the year one thousand seven hundred and seventy three being then about the age of [blank] go into the Kingdom of France and resided there sometime and until the year one thousand seven hundred and seventy five when he returned to England'.[68]

The case intriguingly linked Owen to the Charpentier family when, in May 1778, he granted a £1,200 mortgage to his lawyer, George Morgan, for the benefit of 'Madame Élie Charlotte Charpentier, wife of the Sieur Charpentié, Écuyer du Roi de l'Académie Royalle de Lyon', for 'her sole and separate use notwithstanding her coverture'.[69] Mme Charpentier never cashed in anything, being unaware of the deed. After her death, the fund was lost sight of and got into Chancery,[70] as Walter Scott wrote in his *Journal* (3 May 1826) after he first heard of it in November 1826,[71] a few months after Charlotte's death. Biographers of Scott – Grierson (1938), Edgar Johnson (1970), and John Sutherland (1995) – seized upon the mystery of this bequest and evoked a probable love affair between Welsh pupil Owen and the director's wife. Yet, proof of this extramarital relationship is missing,[72] and, as Sutherland added, 'the Charpentiers still seem to have been living together a year after Owen's death'[73] – that is, in 1781, so that there was no break-up of the household.

Beyond mingling with international students like Owen, the Charpentiers hosted guests from abroad, such as Anglo-Irish inventor Richard Lovell Edgeworth. He stayed with the Charpentiers for two years from autumn 1771 until March 1773, while collaborating with Antoine-Michel Perrache, a sculptor and engineer from Lyon, on a proposal to move the confluence of the Saone and

---

[67] *The Eton College Register*, 1921: 402.
[68] 'Owen v. Morgan b.r.', 18 Oct. 1782, C12/1670/15–18.
[69] Deed of Release, Mrs Isabella Carpenter to Mrs Ann Barlow, 2 Apr. 1833. Reference DD/TP/11, 'Henry Tripp papers', 1756–1832, Somerset Heritage Centre.
[70] References to the funds are made in *The Journal of Sir Walter Scott*, entries 22 Mar. 1826, 3 May 1826, 16 Nov. 1826. Anderson, 1972: 138, 161, 273.
[71] He '[h]ad an account of the claim arising on the estate of one Mrs Owen due to the representatives of my poor wife's mother. [Mr Handley, a solicitor of the old school and manager of the Downshire property] was desperately excursive and spoke almost for an hour but the prospect of £4000 to my children made me a patient auditor', Anderson, 1972: 272–273.
[72] It is not impossible that Charlotte's mother had a short love affair with Owen even though she was not known as his mistress. His mistress was his servant, Maria Seaborn, with whom he had two illegitimate children, Charles and Elizabeth, as declared in his will, written on 19 February 1779, 'Will of Wyrriott Owen, Esq.', SD/1780/200, Department of Collection Services, National Library of Wales.
[73] Sutherland, 1995: 59–60.

the Rhone southwards. Charlotte Charpentier is not mentioned in his *Memoirs*, but that is not surprising considering she was barely one year old. Edgeworth wrote: 'I lodged myself in excellent and cheerful apartments upon the ramparts. I boarded in the family of a gentleman who was at the head of the Military Academy at Lyons, where I soon learned to speak French, so as to be intelligible.'[74] Edgeworth's satisfaction with being 'intelligible' rather than fluent suggests that the Charpentier household was bilingual, with a mix of French and English, a language that Jean Charpentier mastered from his many years abroad:

> M. Charpentier, who was the master of the Academy at Lyons, had seen much of the world, and communicated agreeably what he had seen. He had been controller of the household to the embassy at Constantinople for upwards of twenty years, and had been no inattentive observer. I remember distinctly his having mentioned to me many things relative to Turkey, which I afterwards read in de Tott's Memoirs; and which I heard condemned in de Tott as travellers' wonders. Mad^{me}. Charpentier was young, beautiful, lively, and accomplished, of an excellent disposition, and less fond of publick amusements than most French women. During nearly two years that I was at Lyons, I never had occasion to repent my having established myself in their family, as I met with uniform kindness and confidence from every part of it. I had letters of introduction from several quarters, which made me soon acquainted with the houses, where strangers were received.[75]

Charlotte Charpentier thus grew up in an influential French family, mingling with international students and guests through the Academy of Equitation and her father's connections in high places and position as the king's equerry. The Charpentier household was frequented by British travellers stopping for extended periods, like Edgeworth, as well as Grand Tour tourists passing through Lyon for a few days. Sutherland was surprised by this 'oddity', which can, however, be explained.[76]

At the turn of the eighteenth century and before the French Revolution, Lyon had a strong reputation as a central marketplace, but its identity extended beyond trade and banking. As a city of passage on the Grand Tour, Lyon welcomed a steady stream of foreign travellers and cultural enthusiasts who were recovering after crossing the Alps. Notable visitors included English aristocrat Lady Mary Wortley Montagu,[77] the Duke and Duchess of Cumberland,[78] Prince Henry, Anne Horton, and *salonnière* Hester Lynch

---

[74] Edgeworth and Edgeworth, 1820: 166.   [75] Edgeworth and Edgeworth, 1820: 167–168.

[76] 'One of the oddities about the Charpentier household is that it seems to have been much frequented by British tourists,' Sutherland, 1995: 59–60.

[77] 'I am impatient to see the curiosities of this famous city, and more impatient to continue my journey to Paris,' Montagu, 1820: 73.

[78] Piozzi, 1789: 33.

Thrale during her three-year Grand Tour (1784–1787). Though Lyon lacked a permanent foreign community, these transient visitors relied on recommendations, frequenting the same landmarks and accommodations. Alongside popular choices like Hôtel de la Croix de Malte for Hester Lynch Piozzi and Edward Rigby, or Hôtel d'Artois for English writer Mariana Starke, the Charpentier household was a highly recommended stop.[79] Known for its connections and hospitality, it placed young Charlotte, until the age of seven, in an international and intellectual milieu – what Edgeworth called 'the court of Lyon'.[80]

In addition to socialising with prominent foreigners, the Charpentiers had extensive and influential French contacts throughout the city that later served the Scotts. Such notable connection was the Protestant Delessert family, renowned in trade and banking. Jean-Jacques Delessert had established a successful silk business in Lyon in 1721 and his son, Étienne, expanded into finance in Paris, managing the Caisse d'Escompte – a model for the Banque de France – and founding the first insurance company. Étienne and the Charpentiers shared Parisian roots, a strong interest in education, and the Protestant faith, as Charlotte's mother, Marguerite Charpentier, had raised both her children in this religion. Etienne's philanthropic work, including free schools for Protestant children in the seventh district of Paris, connected him with Edgeworth, also a major figure in the history of education, who had stayed with the Charpentiers through the Delesserts. The Delesserts and the Edgeworths were thus part of Charlotte's social circle from childhood, especially as Étienne's son, Benjamin, born in 1773, was three years younger than her and spent much of his youth in England and Scotland. Scott connected with both the Delesserts and Edgeworths through Charlotte's international network, visiting a school in Edgeworthstown with Wordsworth and meeting the Delesserts during his two trips to Paris.[81]

2.2 A Worldy International Circle on the Wane

This enduring bond was highlighted by Maria Edgeworth, Edgeworth's eldest daughter,[82] when travelling on the Continent almost fifty years after her father. Much to her dismay, during a one-day stop in Lyon on 22 October 1820, she realised that his old acquaintances were no more:

> Lyons! Is it possible that I am really at Lyons, of which I have heard my father speak so much? Lyons! where his active spirit once reigned, and where now scarce a trace, a memory of him remains. The Perraches all gone, Carpentiers

---

[79] Starke, 1802: 7.   [80] Edgeworth and Edgeworth, 1820: 168–169.   [81] Taylor, 1986: 27–50.
[82] Maria Edgeworth is fondly referred to as 'The Great Maria' by Walter Scott, and he openly acknowledges her influence. They corresponded a lot and she spent two weeks with the Scotts in 1823. Johnson, 1970: 138–155.

no more to be heard of, Bons a name unknown; De la Verpilliere – one descendant has a fine house here, but he is in the country.[83]

This letter, sent to her half-sister Honora Edgeworth, stresses Lyon's dramatic transformation. It particularly notes the disappearance of the leading family dynasties from the turn of the century. The surname 'Carpentiers', mentioned here by Maria Edgeworth, is a creative amalgamation; it refers to the Charpentiers, but combines the original French family name with its anglicised translation, 'Carpenters'.

The wealthy society hereupon described, fully collapsing after the French Revolution, was already on the wane in the 1780s. When Jean Charpentier started directing the Academy, with his wife likely teaching some of the optional courses, it was undergoing a period of decline. Previously thriving under Claude Bourgelat from 1740 to 1765, during which time young Charpentier served as master of arms (1743–1755), the Academy struggled under his successor, Dominique-Antoine Payr-Morello. During his six-year tenure (1765–1771), the buildings fell into disrepair, preventing the housing of boarders and likely leading to Payr-Morello's resignation in 1771:[84]

> The proposed successor was Charpentier, a former pupil of Bourgelat, protected by Comte de Vergennes, whom he had accompanied on his embassy to Constantinople. This proposal was accepted and, on 1 March 1771, Charpentier received letters of provision appointing him as an academic squire for the city of Lyon, in place of Payr-Morello, who had resigned.[85]

'Bourgelat's direction had been the academy's shining period; after him it was nothing but a period of decadence that lasted until 1789.'[86] At the Royal Academy of Equitation, the decreasing number of pupils was caused by the dilapidated state of the buildings. In 1775, Jean Charpentier had ordered some expensive repairs and invested a significant amount of money, which the City Council refused to cover, leaving him heavily in debt.[87] Moreover, the Academy was facing growing competition from an expanding number of schools. Lyon was indeed filled with 'excellent masters of all sorts', to take

---

[83] Hare, 2005.
[84] See *Almanach civil, politique et littéraire de Lyon et du département du Rhône*, 1743: 107. The 1743 almanac reveals that the Academy included two masters of arms (one being eighteen-year-old Charpentier), a maths and French teacher, a language instructor for Italian and Spanish, a drawing teacher, a vocal and instrumental music teacher, a dancing tutor, and a writing instructor.
[85] My translation, Duplessis, 1892: 365.
[86] My translation, Duplessis, 1892: 364. The Lyon Royal Academy was successively directed by de Floratil, C. Bourgelat, P. Budin d'Eperville, C. C. Budin, D. D. Payr-Morello, J. Charpentier, Vial, M. de Pavari, and Berthaud.
[87] Dexter, 1960: 147.

up Edgeworth's words, and their numbers kept on growing from the late 1770s into the early 1780s, especially from 1777 when Charpentier's former deputy riding master, Fillion, opened a rival institution.[88] This clandestine riding school was ultimately shut down after eight years by Charles-Eugène de Lorraine, Prince de Lambesc and Grand Squire of France, a supporter of Charpentier. Yet the harm was done; the Academy had been depleted of its pupils, and by 1783, Jean was bankrupt. 'Charpentier's management was extremely turbulent, and it can be said that from that moment on, the life of the Academy was nothing but a series of struggles in which he did not always play the noble part.'[89]

Financially unable to support his family and alarmed by the increasingly hostile political climate towards royal institutions and officials, he found himself at a dead end. He sent his wife as an emissary to plead his cause in Paris, as proved by this translated extract from his unpunctuated letter dated 8 March 1777:[90]

> Let me know if you have any hopes about the pension/ if you see M. Vergenne / you are on the spot/ do your utmost for the success of my requests and I cannot repeat too often hasten your departure/ we will live without seeing company while waiting till our affairs are straightened out/ your children talk only of you/ they are impatient to see you and they kiss you while waiting for your arrival.[91]

Dexter suggests that the 'pension' mentioned here could refer to the funds given by former Academy student Wyrriott Owen to Marguerite Charpentier, particularly the £250 granted to her through a bill of exchange on 13 July 1778. This donation was made just three days before he conveyed all his property to trustees for the benefit of his creditors. Indeed, Owen, being of a spendthrift nature, had been piling up debts since 1773 when he first went abroad. As stated in the Chancery papers, 'That the said Wyrriot Owen having whilst abroad entered into an expensive way of life he was obliged to draw on England for large sums of money considerably more than the annual income of his fortune.'[92] By 1778, he was heavily in debt, especially because while he was in Paris in 1777 and the early months of 1778, he had expended large sums of money on improvements to his estate, which he had inherited roofless and in a state of disrepair. As Marguerite was conducting financial negotiations for her husband with Charles Gravier, comte de Vergennes, and the

---

[88] Edgeworth and Edgeworth, 1820: 166. No trace of this M. Fillion has been found either at the Archives du département du Rhône et de la Métropole de Lyon or at the Archives Municipales de Lyon. See 7C80 in archives.rhone.fr/media/1bbe66d5-e9d2-4f4e-9c60-1e71376a1d9c.pdf.
[89] My translation, Duplessis, 1892: 365.   [90] I have added slashes in the letter for clarity.
[91] Dexter, 1960: 147. Unfortunately, she provides no further reference and I have not yet been able to locate the original letter.
[92] Owen v. Morgan b.r., 18 Oct. 1782, C12/1670/15–18, London National Archives. It shows that six debts secured by mortgage totalled in round numbers £12,000 of principal, Madame Charpentier's being the sixth. Then followed nine debts on bond, which came to £5,600 of principal.

Grand Squire of France, Charles-Eugène de Lorraine, Prince de Lambesc, it is possible – though not provable – that she also negotiated with Owen, then also in Paris, whether he had been her lover or not. In any case, for him to arrange for the £250 note to be given to her just a few days before he went into bankruptcy, he must have felt a strong sense of obligation.[93]

However, it is evident that Marguerite's negotiations in 1777 and again in 1779 were largely unsuccessful and she was recalled home when her husband fell ill. His situation was so precarious, both healthwise and financially, that he faced the serious threat of arrest for debt. From 1777 until he effectively stopped managing the Academy in 1783, his only option was to reluctantly attempt selling it, or what was left of it, to repay his debts, while seeking assistance first from his wife's family and then from the Charpentiers' international friends. In his will, he appointed his friend Arthur Hill, an Irish peer and MP, as trustee and guardian of his widow, son, and daughter. Lockhart's claim, echoed by other critics, that Charpentier had invested '£4,000 in English securities – part in a mortgage upon Lord Downshire's estates' – seems highly improbable.[94]

During a very chaotic four-year period, Jean lost his good reputation with the Prince de Lambesc and more money after a deal with a swindler named Ricard. This ultimately led to the sale of the Academy's equipment to mitigate further losses. Jean officially resigned in 1787, with Payr-Morello taking over for two years until the Academy was abolished by the decrees of the Constituante in 1789.[95]

2.3 Years of Transition

From the age of seven, Charlotte lived in a crumbling household. The Lyon Royal Academy had diminished to a mere shadow of its former self, becoming a blight and a millstone around her father's neck. Her family was broken, with her mother often away for negotiations. The exact timing of the Charpentiers' partial relocation from Lyon to Paris, where they stayed with Marguerite's relatives, remains unclear. There is no mention of Marguerite in Lyon after February 1780. Further details are given by Dexter:

> At the spring of 1782, M. Charpentier had quarantined off epidemics in the school caused by insanitary conditions. During these epidemics, Élie might have taken her children to her mother's in Paris. Again, in the summer of the same year, when Jean was urged to resign, he refused, saying that although he was willing to leave the school temporarily he would not give up his living

---

[93] Dexter, 1960: 170.   [94] Lockhart, 1837–1838: 267; Wright, 1932: 96.
[95] Procès-verbaux des séances des Corps municipaux de la ville de Lyon, 1899: 11–12. See also *Almanach astronomique et historique de la ville de Lyon*, 1788: 226.

quarters. This suggests that the family was away, but that he was expecting, or at least hoping, for their return.[96]

Sources, including Martin-Basse's 1932 reports, lack precise and solid evidence. However, St Eustache parish documents confirm that Mme Charpentier and her children were in Paris by the autumn of 1784.[97] She may have left as early as 1780 with her children when their living conditions became too unsanitary and the financial situation too critical. This would explain why Charlotte wrote in her 25 October 1797 letter to Scott: 'I had the misfortune of losing my father when very young, before I was old enough to know the value of such a parent.'[98] The loss she mentioned might refer to their separation rather than his death. Even if Jean visited them in Paris a few times, she would not have seen him much after their move, and she would have been only ten years old by then.

While in Paris, 'unfortunate Mme Charpentier' lived in a dire state of poverty as reported by Abbé de Chazelle in a letter (Figures 4 and 5) written from 5 rue Favart in Paris, 29 March 1792, and sent to their trustee, Arthur Hill, in Hanover Square, London. Though supported by Arthur Hill, she found herself in a position where she had to 'have her daughter's effects sold' and borrow money to cover her various expenses – clothing, upholstery, a watch chain for her son, and wine – all of which she was unable to repay.[99] Abbé de Chazelle described her as 'often ill or without money' in his letter, corroborating the details in Grierson's biography of Scott: '[i]n fact the unfortunate Madame Charpentier's life was over before the Revolution had, properly speaking, begun'.[100] There are no records of the deaths of Jean Charpentier or Marguerite Charpentier in Lyon, Paris, or England. Destroyed in the fires of the Commune in May 1871, the Paris civil registry prior to 1860 has only been partially reconstructed. Of the 8 million records lost, only a third have been recovered, and their death certificates are not among them.[101] The only certainty is that she died a widow and social outcast,

---

[96] Dexter, 1960: 151. [97] Martin-Basse, 1932: 2.
[98] 'Letters chiefly of Sir Walter Scott, 1792–1817'. [99] Johnson, 1970: 51.
[100] Grierson, 1938: 53. See also 'Lockhart's account of Mme Charpentier as a French Royalist fleeing the Revolution with her children is now known to be an invention,' Daiches, 1971: 55.
[101] Critics have claimed, without providing concrete evidence, that Madame Charpentier's death occurred sometime between 1788, as noted by the *Oxford Dictionary of National Biography*, and 1790, according to Rogers, despite a general consensus that she died after her husband. 'Hence on the death of the widow of M. Charpentier, which happened about the year 1790', Rogers, 1877: lxiv–lxv. I thought I had found proof that she died on 22 November 1788, since there is a death certificate in the name of 'Margueritte Charpentier', who died on that date at the 'Hôpital de la Salpétrière', which, until the French Revolution, served not as a medical facility but as the world's largest hospice. It was a place of exclusion and punishment for women (Carrez, 2008), exclusively used for the confinement of beggars and vagrants. However, upon closer examination, this appears to be a case of mistaken identity, as the associated death record shows that this Margueritte Charpentier was married to Antoine Songeux. Moreover, death certificates are traditionally listed under individuals' maiden names, and there is nothing under the name Volère – regardless of how

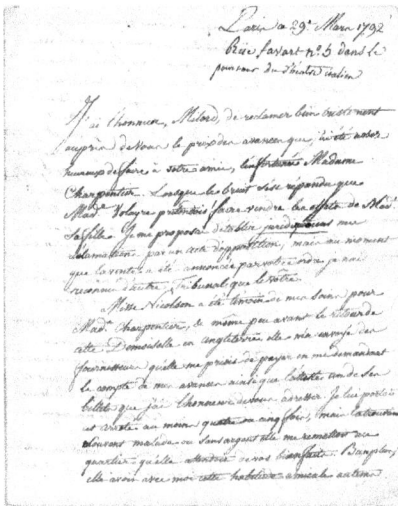

Figure 4 Letter (p. 1) by Abbé de Chazelle, 'Letters chiefly of Sir Walter Scott, 1792–1817'. Image of MS. 2525, used with permission from the National Library of Scotland.

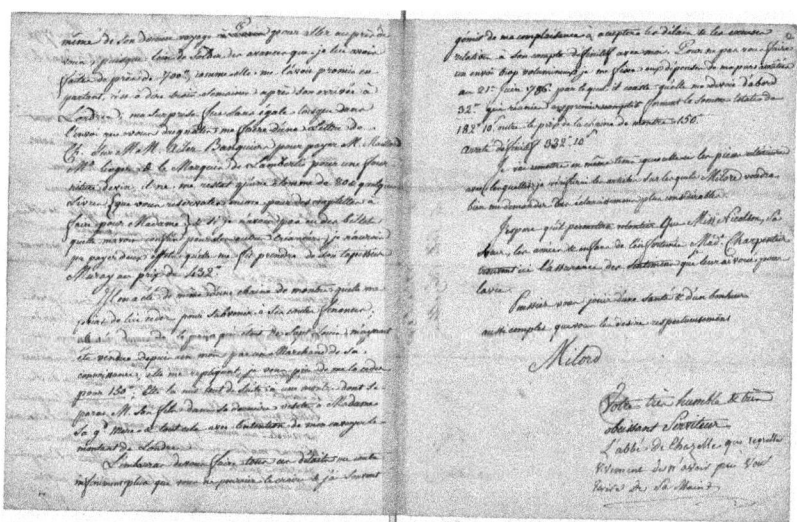

Figure 5 Letter (pp. 2–3) by Abbé de Chazelle, 'Letters chiefly of Sir Walter Scott, 1792–1817'. Image of MS. 2525, used with permission from the National Library of Scotland.

while her husband died sometime after 7 February 1787 – the date he resigned from the Academy – and before her death.

Charlotte Charpentier was thus left an orphan whose identity had shifted dramatically – from wealth to poverty and from living in the household of an influential royal official to that of political and social pariahs – with her father's loss of support from the grand squire of France and the whole family becoming marginalised. No wonder she was reluctant to talk about her childhood when she met Scott. Thus ungrounded by her family's misfortunes, she became uprooted in England where she had to learn how to unbecome French.

3 Unbecoming French: Charlotte's Shifting Identity in Cosmopolitan London

3.1 Charlotte's Fabricated Identity in Her London Foster Home

Charlotte Charpentier and her brother, Charles, moved to London sometime after the autumn of 1784. They 'were recorded as living in Hanover Square in London in 1785, possibly in 1784 and definitely in 1787',[102] Kirsty Carpenter indicated in her book *Refugees of the French Revolution*.[103] Tracing the Charpentiers' arrival in England is challenging because the Aliens' Entry Book at the London National Archives only begins in 1794, and census records start even later, from 1841.[104] Yet, despite the absence of authentic official documents, there are a few clues to help pinpoint the timing of their transnational move.

After relocating, whether temporarily or permanently, from Lyon to Paris around 1780, Madame Charpentier and her children lived with a certain 'Miss Nicolson', as evidenced by the aforementioned letter from Abbé de Chazelle: 'Miss Nicolson witnessed the care I provided for Mad^e Charpentier,' the abbot wrote in 1792.[105] Miss Nicolson did not enter the service of the Charpentiers until after September 1784, however. Jane Nicolson, the youngest

---

the surname is spelt. See https://archives.paris.fr/s/5/etat-civil-reconstitue-fichiers/resultats, 'État civil', 'État civil reconstitué (18e–1859)', 'Fichiers de l' État civil reconstitué', 'décès: Charpentier', V3E/D272, and https://archives.paris.fr/s/39/etat-civil-reconstitue-actes/resultats/?, with the corresponding death certificate being in the first batch (5Mi1 1127), on page 44 of the viewer.

[102] Carpenter, 1999: 40, note 36.

[103] This contradicts other more fanciful accounts, like Bigger's: 'Madame Carpentier found out Lord Hillsborough, and was sheltered by him in his mansion in Burlington Street until other arrangements were made,' Bigger, 1922.

[104] https://discovery.nationalarchives.gov.uk/details/r/C4286474; www.nationalarchives.gov.uk/help-with-your-research/research-guides/census-records.

[105] My translation, 'Miss Nicolson a été témoin de mes soins pour Mad^e Charpentier' (see aforementioned letter). He went on discussing the young lady's return to England: 'peu avant le retour de cette Demoiselle en Angleterre' (shortly before the return of that lady [*demoiselle* – i.e. Miss Nicolson] to England', my translation).

of three daughters of Dr Nicolson, Dean of Exeter, had indeed been chosen by Welsh writer and socialite Esther Thrale in June 1784, when, causing much uproar at the time, Thrale had left England without her children, who disapproved of her remarriage to the family's music teacher.[106] 'Mrs Thrale tried to locate a proper chaperone for the girls. She had considerable difficulty finding the right person, but in the end settled upon a mature woman of fashion, kindly but correct, Miss Jane Nicolson, a daughter of the Dean of Exeter who gave James Evans of Southwark as a reference.'[107] Yet Jane's tenure as a chaperone for the Thrale children was short-lived; she was dismissed three months later, so that in September 1784 she was free to be hired as the governess for both Charpentier children, with the additional role of chaperone for Charlotte.[108] Her presence in Paris is proved by Abbé de Chazelle's letter, and confirmed by Scott himself in two letters. In the first, dated 12 November 1827, to his son-in-law Lockhart, he wrote, '[s]he came from France with Made. Charpentier and her children'.[109] In the second letter, from 10 January 1828, to his son Charles, Scott, having finally decided to inquire into his late wife's origins, stated, 'Miss Jane Nicolson is the only person I know who can explain the circumstances of Mrs. Charpentier's coming to England, as she was with her at the time.'[110] With both parents destitute and ill – their father staying in Lyon, busy trying to sell the Academy until 1787, and their mother living with what was left of her family in Paris before possibly ending up in a hospice or such like – the Charpentier children were indeed in need of a governess and chaperone. Now, why the move to England?

First of all, with Jean Charpentier's loss of support in the highest circles of power and his half-hearted efforts to sell the Academy of Equitation, which had completely lost its prestige under his leadership – though he was not entirely to blame – the family had become social and political outcasts, especially in the unstable and uncertain pre-Revolutionary French context. Despite unproven rumors of his wife's infidelity, it is quite likely, though unconfirmed, that Jean Charpentier approved of his children moving to England. Moreover, it was illegal for children to leave the country without their father's consent. Leaving France and adopting new identities was, he probably thought, the best option for their future. Moving abroad to erase the past and start with a clean slate, unrooting them, was a necessary step for their potential growth. Whether they

---

[106] Balderston, 1942: 599 and Petty-Fitzmaurice, 1934: 137–185.
[107] Hyde, 1977: 240. 'On the following morning [25 June 1784] Mrs Thrale, Miss Nicolson, and the three girls drove to Wilton and Fonthill, viewing pictures and sights, and then on to Salisbury, where they parted, midway between their two destinations, so that no one later could accuse either party of desertion. Miss Nicolson and the girls proceeded to the West Street house in Brighton, and Mrs Thrale returned to Bath, to await the arrival of Piozzi.'
[108] 'They went to Brighton and dismissed the woman. The girls were adrift,' Hyde, 1977: 242.
[109] Grierson, 1932–1937: X:310.   [110] Grierson, 1932–1937: X:359.

went with their father's consent or not, however, their departure was no part of an elopement. Instead, their mother, accompanied by Jane Nicolson, took them to England, and once the children were comfortably settled in their new foster home, the two women returned to France.[111]

England, particularly London, was a relatively common destination for many, especially French-speaking Protestants with artisanal and artistic skills, who had been fleeing politico-religious upheavals on the Continent since the annulment of the Edict of Nantes in 1685.[112] Between 1550 and 1800, around 65,000 French-speaking Protestants had come to London as refugees and many had established influential communities there.[113] Though baptised as Catholics at the Abbaye d'Ainay in Lyon, just one hundred yards from the Royal Academy of Equitation, Charlotte and her brother 'had been educated in the Protestant religion of their mother'.[114] Mme Charpentier wanted her children to be raised in the Anglican Church, and at that time all forms of Protestant worship were forbidden in predominantly Catholic France. This was another reason she wished to send them to England.

The French-speaking community, which was mostly Protestant until then, grew even larger and more diverse a few years after the arrival of the Charpentier children in the 1790s. This was because émigrés were escaping the French Revolution, and London – just thirty hours from Paris – became a convenient and attractive refuge for French royalists.[115] Although it is clear that the Charpentiers were not refugees of the French Revolution,[116] and 'were not victims of the Terror, there is evidence to suggest that he [Jean Charpentier] sent his family to London in order to avoid the coming political and economic storm'.[117] England emerged as a better alternative when France became synonymous with a shameful past, marked by the family's downfall, and a bleak future with no prospects.

Besides, most of the Charpentiers' network was international, as studied in Section 2. Marguerite and her children sought refuge in England where the family had close connections, starting with Arthur Hill, a 'great friend' of M. Charpentier, as Charlotte stated in her correspondence to Scott on 25 October 1797.[118] Known as Lord Fairford and the future Earl of Hillsborough (1789–1793), Hill later became the Marquess of Downshire after his father's death in 1793, at which time he was also appointed to the

---

[111] Letter by Scott to Lockhart, 14 Nov. 1827 and to his son, 11 Jan. 1828, Grierson, 1932–1937: X:309, 359.
[112] Cornick, 2013: 2.   [113] Cornick, 2013: 1.   [114] Lockhart, 1837–1838: 267.
[115] Carpenter, 1999: 162.
[116] For the differences between refugees and emigrants, see Reboul, 2017: 73–80.
[117] Carpenter, 1999: 163.
[118] 'After my father's death we were left to the care of Lord Downshire, who had been his very great friend,' 'Letters chiefly of Sir Walter Scott, 1792–1817'; Lockhart, 1837–1838: 278.

Privy Council of Ireland. Lockhart described the meeting between Arthur Hill and the Charpentiers as follows: 'the late Marquis of Downshire . . . had, in the course of his travels in France, formed an intimate acquaintance with the family, and, indeed, spent some time under their roof',[119] an account supported by Reverend Roger,[120] a nineteenth-century Scottish minister and prolific author. Critics remain divided on the timing of Hill's possible visit to France. According to the Dictionary of Irish Biography, he matriculated at Magdalen College, Oxford, on 18 May 1771, and graduated with an MA on 9 July 1773.[121] Martin Davis noted that '[f]ollowing study at Oxford, he [Hill] does not appear to have made the Grand Tour'.[122] However, a letter from Dr Richard Starke to Hill's father dated 22 May 1776 (Figures 6 and 7) mentioned 'the precise time that Lord Fairford was abroad is immaterial; but for your Lordship's information otherways, I think Lord Fairford set out from London about 2 o'clock in the afternoon, on Sunday the 1st of August of 1773, and returned to London, about midday, on Wednesday the 25th of January 1775'.[123]

Like his cousin Arthur Wellesley, who attended the Royal Academy of Equitation in Angers, it is very likely that Arthur Hill spent some time at the Lyon institution, even if there is no evidence that his trip abroad included France and specifically Lyon. This can only be a reasonable assumption, not a definitive statement, despite some critics hastily concluding from this letter that these dates coincided with Hill's trip to France.[124] This may have been Hill's first visit, when Charlotte was about two or three years old; other visits likely followed with critics suggesting various dates. Chambers pointed to 1783 in the second article of 'The Land of Scott' series in the *Edinburgh Journal*. Crockett favoured 1786, while Bigger favoured 1788 – Jean Charpentier would have been either dying or recently deceased.[125]

In any case, it seems reasonable to assume that Arthur Hill and Jean Charpentier first met around 1773 when Hill was a student at the Academy. They likely saw each other or corresponded frequently enough afterward to form such a close bond that around 1787, in his will, Jean Charpentier appointed Hill as trustee and guardian of his widow, son, and daughter (see Section 2.2). Hill became extremely powerful and wealthy, especially after marrying Mary Sandys, one of the country's foremost landowners, in June 1786. The long-standing, sincere, and affectionate friendship between the two men, combined

---

[119] Lockhart, 1837–1838: 267.
[120] 'During a Continental tour Lord Hillsborough had become intimately acquainted with the family, and spent some time under their roof,' Rogers, 1877: lxiv–lxv.
[121] Entry 'Hill, Arthur', in Foster, 1888: 659. [122] Davis, 2020: 33.
[123] Letter from Dr Richard Starke to Lord Hillsborough, D607/B/10, Public Record of Northern Ireland (Belfast).
[124] Carswell's quotation in Crockett, 1930b; 'about the year 1773', Oman, 1973: 363.
[125] Quoted in Grierson, 1930.

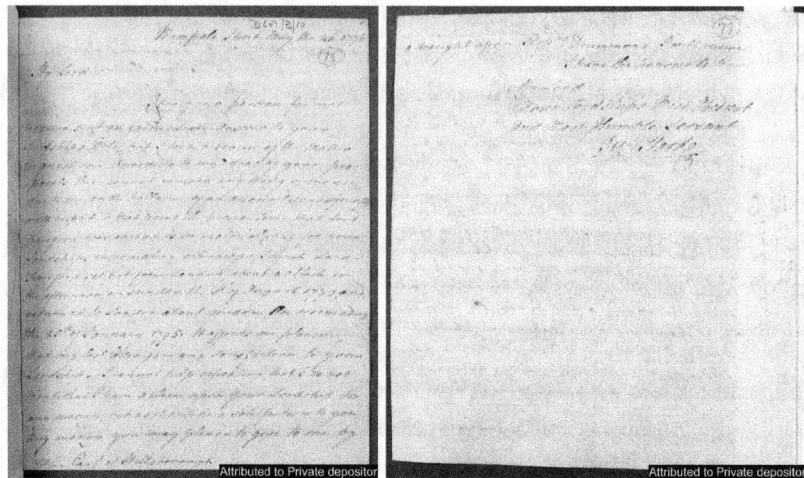

Figures 6 and 7 Dr Richard Starke's letter to Arthur Hill's father, the Earl of Hillsborough, 22 May 1776, credit to the Deputy Keeper of the Records, Public Record Office of Northern Ireland.

with Hill's gratitude to Jean Charpentier for his training at the Academy, his financial comfort, the minimal burden the role posed for him, and the common practice of wealthy men of high rank taking on wards – Scott himself was the guardian of Margaret Clephane and her sister – provide sufficient explanation for why Hill accepted the role of providing financial support and protection for the Charpentier children.[126]

Over the years, critics have speculated more licentious reasons, such as the idea that he was another of Marguerite Charpentier's lovers. However, this theory doesn't hold up when considering M. Charpentier's will and Charlotte's boundless gratitude to her guardian. In her courtship letters to Scott, she wrote that she owed all the good fortune of her life to 'the blessing of having your Lordship for my friend and protector', and she called him 'the very best man on earth'.[127] More recently, in 1960, Dexter came up with yet another intriguing new theory, suggesting that Charlotte's mother might have been Arthur Hill's half-sister instead of his mistress, implying that Charlotte's grandmother had been the mistress of the First Marquess of Downshire, Arthur Hill's father, although she fails to provide evidence to support this hypothesis.[128]

---

[126] Grierson, 1938: 126.
[127] Grierson, 1937–1938, I:123, 302; letter to Scott dated 26 Nov. 1797, 'Letters chiefly of Sir Walter Scott, 1792–1817'.
[128] Dexter, 1960: 173–174.

As the Charpentier children's trustee and guardian, Arthur Hill offered them both financial support and protection, primarily vouching for their social standing and legitimacy. He was the one who had hired Jane Nicolson to care for Marguerite Charpentier and her children in Paris. Thanks to Hill's intervention, Charles, upon arriving in England at the age of twelve, attended a boarding school in Hertford that specialised in preparing pupils for the Indian service. Hill wanted him to secure a profitable position with the East India Company so he could later provide for his sister and make her an attractive match. Yet, for that, he needed a strong command of both spoken and written English. Still thanks to Hill's influence, aged seventeen, he received his appointment on 27 July 1789,[129] and quickly rose through the ranks,[130] eventually serving as Commercial Resident at Salem from 1794 until his death there on 4 June 1818.[131] While Charles attended school,[132] Charlotte lived at Arthur Hill's in Hanover Square; this is where she asked Scott to send his letters during their courtship in 1797: 'Direct to Lord Downshire, Hanover Square, London'.[133]

Both children fully assimilated into London society since, in addition to Charles attending a British school and Charlotte living with an influential and affluent British family, they both changed names and religion. Their identity underwent a voluntary transformative shift as they crossed the Channel. 'Many of the French had of course adopted anglicised versions of their names' when settling in England, Kirsty Carpenter explained, including the Charpentiers.[134] And yet they went beyond just adopting English surnames or English equivalents; they changed their first names entirely, complicating the tracing of their movements.

Charlotte Charpentier, originally christened 'Marguerite' after her mother, adopted her mother's middle name, 'Charlotte', and added 'Sophia' in honour of Antoinette Adélaïde Dumergue, known as 'Sophia', a young French lady of almost her age whom she had befriended in London.[135] So, from 1770 to 1787, she was known as Marguerite Charlotte Charpentier, and after 1787, she adopted the full name Charlotte Sophia Carpenter. Her brother, originally named Jean David, chose the first name Charles – and he will be referred to

---

[129] These specific dates appear in Dexter, 1960: 157–158. In her letter to Scott dated 31 Oct. 1797, Charlotte mentioned that her 'brother has been gone to India only near nine years', which would mean sometime in 1789, 'Letters chiefly of Sir Walter Scott, 1792–1817'.

[130] See Carpenter's entry in *Record of Services of the Honourable East India Company's Civil Servants in the Madras Presidency*, 1885: 22.

[131] See Wright's (1932: 96–97) and Lockhart's (1837–1838: 267) accounts even if both are erroneous.

[132] In June 1787, he was transferred to a day school founded by a Frenchman half a mile's walk from the Dumergues, at 10 Burlington Street, off Piccadilly, Richardson 2000: 187.

[133] Charlotte's letter to Walter Scott, 7 Oct. 1797, 'Letters chiefly of Sir Walter Scott, 1792–1817'.

[134] Carpenter, 1999: 160.

[135] See her baptismal certificate at Ainay (register No. 349), Archives de Lyon: 326.

as Charles in this Element from now on – inspired by Charles François Dumergue, the father of Sophia, with whom the siblings sometimes stayed in London. Interestingly, both children reshaped their identities by borrowing names from the Dumergues, a French-born, French-speaking family based in London, who will be the focus of Section 3.2. They twisted their French roots and fabricated a new British identity by associating with a French family who had successfully moved to England and become extremely wealthy and influential in London – a reverse image of their own biological family, or, rather, what the Charpentiers could have become had history taken a different course.

In any case, this fabricated ancestry and borrowed heritage ultimately erased their true background, a process further reinforced by the fact that, along with being rechristened, the Charpentier children also officially converted to Protestantism, distancing them even more from their birth country. Aged seventeen and fifteen, about three years after their exile, they joined the Anglican Church at George's Church, Hanover Square, London, on 13 May 1787.[136] This was the Dumergues' parish church, and eighteen-year-old Sophia Dumergue was baptised alongside them, further strengthening the sentimental, rather than blood, bond between the two families. For Charlotte, it was a kind of spiritual and identity rebirth in a new country, with an idealised, recreated French-born family.

What is particularly interesting about her northward journey from France to Britain in 1784 is that Charlotte represents a still underexplored group – those who settled in Britain well before the watershed moment of 1789.[137] Arriving almost five years earlier, she came as a voluntary migrant rather than as a refugee.[138]

---

[136] Pope-Hennessy, 1932: 30–31.

[137] Quite a few books have been dedicated to the French Huguenots (Irene Scouloudi's 1987 *Huguenots in Britain and Their French Background, 1550–1800*; Robin Gwynn's 1983 'The Number of Huguenot Immigrants in England, 1680–1700' and 1985 *Huguenot Heritage: The History and Contribution of the Huguenots in Britain*; David J. B. Trim's 2011 *The Huguenots: History and Memory in Transnational Context*); or to the refugees of the French Revolution in London (Kirsty Carpenter's 1999 *Refugees of the French Revolution: Émigrés in London, 1789–1802*; Kirsty Carpenter and Philip Mansel's 1999 *The French Émigrés in Europe and the Struggle against Revolution, 1789–1814*; Juliette Reboul's 2017 *French Emigration to Great Britain in Response to the French Revolution* or Juliette Reboul and Laure Philip's 2019 *French Emigrants in Revolutionised Europe*). See bibliography for further references on this topic, but there is little research on the more diverse profiles of individuals who travelled to Britain in the intervening period. Only French visitors to Britain have been studied – for example, Gerbod's 1995 *Les Voyageurs Français à la découverte des Iles Britanniques du 18e siècle à nos jours* and Gury's 1999 *Le Voyage outre-manche: anthologie de voyageurs français de Voltaire à Mac Orlan*.

[138] 'She was the daughter of a wealthy member of the new nobility in Lyon and although they were not victims of the Terror there is evidence to suggest that he sent his family to London in order to avoid the coming political and economic storm,' Carpenter, 1999: 163. Carpenter identifies four waves of emigration. The first, in July 1789, following the outbreak of the Revolution, saw rural aristocrats fleeing peasant uprisings. The second, after Louis XVI's failed escape in 1791, involved members of the upper classes. The third and most substantial wave came after the

Had she been a refugee, she might have tried and returned to France during one of several windows of opportunity, as explained by historian Friedemann Pestel:[139] either in late 1791 – a brief period when returning carried no legal consequences – or after the Terror in 1794–1795, when Robespierre's fall led to a relaxation of émigré laws and fewer deportations or even much later in March 1802, once the Peace of Amiens was signed.[140]

In fact, she falls outside any established category, belonging to neither of the two main waves of French emigration at the time: the first, a large movement of Huguenots – skilled artisans, traders, professionals such as doctors, and intellectuals – who fled religious persecution between 1680 and 1750; and the second, a more limited wave of nobles, royalists, refractory priests, and intellectuals who settled temporarily in London from 1788 onwards, drawn by its vibrant cultural and political life while fleeing the Terror and revolutionary upheaval in France. Her transnational move closely resembled that of the Huguenots, echoing their patterns of assimilation and settlement, though it was driven by different purposes and occurred out of sync with that historical wave. Like many Huguenots, she assimilated, anglicised her name – from Charpentier to Carpenter – to ease her integration, and she never returned to France, not even accompanying her husband on his two visits to her mother country. She settled in Hanover Square, part of the City of Westminster – at the time a prestigious, affluent address favoured by wealthy and aristocratic residents – where French Huguenots had earlier taken refuge. They had settled in this London district as well as Soho, Hammersmith, and Spitalfields.

Charlotte's move thus fell outside the major, well-defined waves of emigration. She was part of a more heterogeneous group belonging to the French elite who migrated to London for reasons that were social, political, educational, scientific, or cultural – rather than in direct response to major historical upheavals.[141] This group's mobility was often facilitated – as in Charlotte's case – by existing networks of family and friends already living in Britain. Figures like Benjamin Delessert spent several years studying in England, where he met leading thinkers such as Adam Smith and witnessed a demonstration of the steam engine by James Watt. He also encountered Jean-André Deluc in

---

storming of the Tuileries and the September Massacres in 1792. The last one, in March–April 1793, was triggered by harsh legislation that declared émigrés legally dead, stripped them of their citizenship, confiscated their property, and made emigration a capital offence.

[139] 'The large majority of émigrés aimed to return to France at their earliest convenience; and this convenience was largely a political one', Pestel, 2019: 211.

[140] Carpenter, 1999: xix; Kelly and Cornick, 2013.

[141] The London Royal Society served as a key point of reference for French scientists at the time. Coquillard, 2020: 39.

Windsor, who introduced him to the latest developments in geology. Others, like Charles Alexandre de Calonne – Louis XVI's finance minister, nicknamed 'Monsieur Déficit' – settled in London in 1787 for both personal and political reasons. Accused of financial misconduct, he relocated to Hyde Park Corner with his brother, Abbé de Calonne.

Charlotte's migration, then, aligns more with this discrete yet influential pattern of elite mobility, driven by individual trajectories rather than revolutionary rupture. It shows that émigré agency did 'overcome the older dichotomy of voluntary vs. involuntary migration, a somewhat nostalgic victimisation, and an emphatic perspective on émigré "activism"'.[142] Charlotte's migration was of a very different nature. She could have found herself in Britain – and in a position, socially speaking, to meet Scott – through her own international family connections in London, and even more so thanks to their overlapping social circles and mutual acquaintances. The Nicolsons and the Birds, Jane Nicolson's cousins, shared friends with Walter Scott. While the French Revolution may have offered a convenient backdrop, it was by no means essential to her move.

3.2 Charlotte at the Dumergues': A Spitting Image of the Charpentiers before the Fall

Once Arthur Hill was married and from 1787, Charlotte Charpentier often stayed with the Dumergues at 118 New Bond Street, Westminster.[143] Originally from France and French-speaking, Charles Dumergue 'had been intimately acquainted with the Charpentiers in his own early life in France, and had warmly befriended Mrs Scott's mother on her first arrival in England', as Lockhart stated, though no further details are provided.[144] 'His [Charles Dumergue's] family appears to have had important connections with the French court at its higher levels,' which could explain why Charles Dumergue might have earlier interacted with the Charpentiers in France, with Marguerite belonging to an old French house in Paris and Jean serving as a key official, the controller to the household, in the 1750s and 1760s.[145] However, no proof of their acquaintance or the context of their interactions has been found.

---

[142] Pestel, 2019: 211.

[143] This address appears on the letters Charlotte sent to Charles Dumergue or his daughter. See letters dated 10 Dec. 1797 to Charles and 29 Apr. 1798 to Sophia in 'Letters chiefly of Sir Walter Scott, 1792–1817'. Dumergue's dentist cabinet was at 32 Old Burlington Street, also in the Mayfair district of Westminster.

[144] Lockhart, 1837–1838: 372.   [145] Beauchamp, 2012: 3.

After marrying in 1763, Charles's dental practice could no longer support the couple's genteel lifestyle in Paris. This prompted their emigration to England, as his ex-wife attested in her petition stored in the Parliamentary Archives:[146]

> Immediately after the said marriage the said Charles François and your Petitioner lived at Paris but the said Charles François could not acquire practice in his profession there by any means adequate to a genteel support of himself and your Petitioner, and that during the time they continued to live in France which was about three years after their marriage your Petitioner earned the chief of their subsistence.
>
> That the said Charles François finding himself incapable of success in France came to London about the year 1766 and here met with every great success insomuch that the said Charles François to the certain knowledge of your petition hath saved several thousand pounds sterling and the said Charles François lives now in a very splendid manner and earns annually on an average from fourteen to sixteen hundred pounds.[147]

Once in London, 'Dumergue was able to build himself a large, flourishing and profitable practice which was eventually based at his home.'[148] It was extremely fashionable for the British upper classes, and the aristocracy in particular, to resort to the services of French physicians, so that Dumergue was not short of work,[149] 'attending on Queen Charlotte and at the teething of some of her fifteen children',[150] before taking up the post of dentist to the Prince of Wales – that is, King George III – from 1785 to his death in 1814.[151] Very popular and well known, he was one of the first to realise the importance to health of good dentistry and he is said to have introduced false teeth in England.

After his sensational divorce, granted by a bill in the House of Lords in 1779,[152] Dumergue lived on New Bond Street – close to Hanover Square, where

---

[146] As indicated by the Parliamentary Archives, they settled in London, living in Bond Street until Dumergue secured another lodging for his wife in Paddington when her health began to deteriorate. She claimed to be suffering from an asthmatic disorder. See Anne Catherine Dumergue's Petition, 5 May 1779, Parliamentary Archives.

[147] 'Petition of Anne Catherine Dumergue', 5 May 1779, reference HL_PO_JO_10_7_596, Parliamentary Archives.

[148] Beauchamp, 2012: 4.

[149] Known as Charles Dumergue of Picadilly, he even had a mechanical assistant, Samuel Cartwright, trained as an ivory turner.

[150] Beauchamp, 2012: 3.   [151] *Bulletin of the History of Dentistry*, 41 (1993), 11.

[152] Charles Dumergue married Anne Catherine Labroue, of Huguenot descent, on 20 June 1763. However, in 1778 she began an affair with a Frenchman, Lazarus Claudius Morlet, whom Dumergue had hired to teach their daughter, Sophia, English and French. Following numerous petitions and testimonies from their servants and other witnesses, a final sentence of separation and divorce was issued on 27 Feb. 1779. Read the witnesses' testimonies: www.british-history.ac.uk/lords-jrnl/vol35/pp767-788. Charles' unfaithful wife was then free to marry her lover at St Mary-Le Bone Church, London, on 24 August 1779. See also 'Dumergue's Divorce Bill', *Journals of the House of Lords*, 35 (1779), 762.

the Hills lived – from 1786 and then from 1800 at 15 Piccadilly West, a prestigious address at the time, home to aristocrats, wealthy merchants, and notable establishments.[153] Aided by his naturalisation as a British citizen in 1793, he had successfully integrated into English society, but he enjoyed mingling with international people and entertained extensively, hosting a large community of French-speaking émigrés – some long established in London, others newly arrived due to the Revolution – as well as prominent German and British men and women.[154] His environment was highly cosmopolitan, typical of a wealthy and fashionable man in the late eighteenth century.

Charlotte's frequent stays at the Dumergues' were due in part to the biological sisterhood between governesses Sarah and Jane – Jane Nicolson's older sister, Sarah, was the Dumergues' housekeeper – as well as the adoptive sisterhood Charlotte shared with Sophia Dumergue, Charles' only daughter, a bond almost sacredly cemented through their shared religious experience of baptism in 1787.[155] Charlotte was known to be a fervent Protestant, much more so than her husband, as Mr Mitchell, a former tutor to the Scotts' children, recounted in words reported in Lockhart's *Memoirs*:

> What constituted her distinguishing ornament was that she was sincerely religious. Some years previous to my entrance into the family, I understood from one of the servants she had been under deep religious concern about her soul's salvation, which had ultimately issued in a conviction of the truth of Christianity, and in the enjoyment of its divine consolations.[156]

This well-integrated French-born family was an opportunity for Charlotte to start anew. The Dumergues were a spitting image of her own family, the Charpentiers, before the Fall. They also started out as a broken family – in the Dumergues' case, due to an unfaithful and later absent mother after the parents' divorce. However, they successfully turned their downfall into something positive and uplifting: a blended, diverse, and joyful family made up of relatives like Charles' nephew – that is, Sophia's cousin Jean Jorlie – who joined them

---

[153] The house number was in fact 96, but it was at no. 15 Piccadilly, West Street.

[154] '(Bill received royal assent 28 Mar., 1793.) ... Charles Francis Dumergue, dentist, son of Francis Dumergue, by Teresa Laidet his wife, born in the Province of Anjoumois in France, but now of the Parish of Saint George, Hanover Square, in the County of Middlesex'. 'Letters of Denisation and Acts of Naturalisation for Aliens in England and Ireland, 1701–1800', *The Publications of the Huguenot Society of London*. Manchester: Sherrat and Hughes, 1923. https://archive.org/stream/lettersofdenizat2717hugu/lettersofdenizat2717hugu_djvu.txt. His middle name is referred to as either François or Francis after he was naturalised.

[155] When going to London, Scott mentions 'visiting the Piccadilly ladies' (*Journal* entry 18 Oct. 1826), meaning 'Miss Antoinette Adelaide Dumergue (known as Sophia) and her housekeeper, Miss Sarah Ann Nicolson (usually given the courtesy of Mrs.), Lady Scott's 'earliest and best friends', *Letters*, xi, 399; Anderson, 1972: 246, note 6.

[156] Lockhart, 1837–1838: 89.

from France in 1790 and became naturalised in March 1793, at the same time as his uncle, taking the name of Charles Joseph Dumergue[157] – and 'adopted' members, like their employee, the housekeeper Sarah Nicolson, nicknamed Sally, whom Sophia regarded as 'more than a mother'.[158] It was a different model of family, centred around a mother figure, with Sophia and Charles as doppelgängers of Charlotte – whose chosen second name, it should be recalled, was Sophia – and her brother, Charles.

I believe that, for Charlotte, this erasure of the Fall had a religious dimension – both the sin and the imperfection that accounted for her family's brokenness. By aligning with the Dumergues, she sought to shed her family's sinful nature and find the redemption she thought the Charpentiers lacked. After losing her blood family, she fully embraced her chosen family, much more so than her brother, Charles, who had arrived in England at a younger age, attended a British school, and became fully integrated, with no trace of foreign idiom or perspective in his letters. Conversely, Charlotte remained emotionally attached and connected to her French roots through the Dumergues, which explains why she retained a French influence throughout her life, an influence that would later have a profitable impact on her husband as her social circle eventually became part of Walter Scott's coterie.

3.3 From Charlotte's Cosmopolitan Circle to Scott's Artistic Coterie

Charles Dumergue and his household, based in the bustling, fashionable district of Westminster, were instrumental in Charlotte Charpentier's social and cultural education – with Dumergue becoming Charlotte's new trustee in November 1801 after Arthur Hill tragically took his own life following the loss of all his government positions – furthering the transnational and transcultural upbringing she had experienced in Lyon.

From age fifteen to twenty-seven, Charlotte Charpentier was thus immersed in a warm, sociable, and international environment even more cosmopolitan than the one she had known in Lyon, with French, German, and English spoken equally in Charles Dumergue's household. Described as 'a Frenchman full of gallic charm', he entertained extensively, so that his daughter, Sophia, with the help of Mrs Nicolson, hosted large salons, dinner parties, and private concerts for eminent literary and scientific men and women.[159] Charlotte was thus 'fashionable, and, to Scott's

---

[157] That is why when writing to Charles Dumergue at 118 New Bond Street on 10 Dec. 1797, Charlotte wrote: 'Will you have the goodness to present our love, and best wishes to your ladies, and Charles, and to tell Miss Dumergue, we have received all the things,' 'Letters chiefly of Sir Walter Scott, 1792–1817'.

[158] Beauchamp, 2012: 5.   [159] Mason, 2005: 87.

delight, gratifyingly well-connected' with her connections regularly benefitting her husband.[160] The first time the Scotts went to the Dumergues' in London was in the spring of 1798: Scott had to see his most important client, the marquis of Abercorn, a mutual intimate acquaintance of both Scott and Charlotte. The marquis and his wife, Anne Jane Hamilton, Lady Abercorn, were friends of Charlotte's guardian, Arthur Hill.[161] The Scotts remained very close to the Dumergues even after Charles Dumergue's death in 1814, often staying at his house – where Sophia and Sarah Nicolson still lived – when they went down to London.[162] Several letters dated 29 March 1803, 24 March 1807, and 8 April 1815 mention either the Scotts or Scott alone going to London and being hosted by the Dumergues.[163] Thanks to Sophia and her housekeeper Sarah, the Dumergues' home continued to serve as a salon: 'Here Scott met much highly interesting French society, and until a child of his own was established in London, he never thought of taking up his abode anywhere else, as often as he had occasion to be in town.'[164] For example, there he met the Duc de Sérent, a French military officer and politician who had lived in London and then Edinburgh before returning to Paris in 1814, serving the elder brother of the king of France, later King Louis XVIII, during his exile in England in 1807. His daughter, Émilie de Sérent, who had been living in London with her husband, the Duc de Narbonne-Pelet, since 1791, was also a frequent visitor at the Dumergues' and a close friend of Charlotte, who was the same age, along with Françoise de Chalus, Comtesse de Narbonne-Lara – a former mistress of Louis XV, who had also fled Paris after the French Revolution. When Scott travelled to Paris in September 1815, accompanied by Sophia Dumergue and Sarah Nicolson, 'our Piccadilly friends'[165] as he would call them – with the possessive 'our' stressing that Charlotte's London friends had become part of his social circle – he was invited to dinner at the Duc de Sérent's.[166] The duke was also a friend of the Boultons, whom Scott met at the Dumergues'. Scott likely considered installing gas lighting – a very new industry in Britain after 1800 – in his home at Abbotsford after conversations at the

---

[160] Dunlop, 2016: 83.
[161] In Scott's letter to Lady Abercorn, 9 June 1806: 'She [Charlotte] has a great remembrance of her late Protector & friend Lord Downshire which extends to all his friends but Lady Abercorn in particular,' Grierson, 1932–1937: X:303.
[162] When going to London, Scott mentions 'visiting the Piccadilly ladies' (entry 18 Oct. 1826), meaning Sophia and Sarah Nicolson, Lady Scott's earliest and best friends; see Anderson, 1972: 246, note 6.
[163] 'Letters chiefly of Sir Walter Scott, 1792–1817'. [164] Lockhart, 1837–1838: 372.
[165] Scott's letter to Charlotte, 13 Sept. 1815, 'Letters chiefly of Sir Walter Scott, 1792–1817'.
[166] 'I saw Mr Duke de Sérent a day before I came away, I was determined to prolong my visit till the last as I did not wish the good old man to bother himself with asking me,' Scott's letter to Charlotte, 13 Sept. 1815, 'Letters of Sir Walter Scott to His Wife on His Travel Plans', Acc. 14307, National Library of Scotland.

Dumergues' with Scottish engineer James Watt and Birmingham manufacturer and engineer Matthew Boulton,[167] whom Scott visited at his home in April 1807.[168]

Although Charlotte did introduce Scott to eminent military leaders, political figures, and scientists, the core of her social circle remained 'Dumergue's many theatrical and artist friends'.[169] Her social network, which likely greatly differed from Scott's more Scottish, politically and legally connected circle, at least until his first publications in the 1810s, was distinguished by its highly international and creative, artistic nature. Among the Dumergue family's frequent dining companions was neoclassical German painter Johan Zoffany or Alsatian-born British painter Philippe-Jacques de Loutherbourg, also known by his Anglicised name as Philip James. The latter had settled in London in 1771 and was renowned not only for his extensive naval works, but also for his intricate set designs at London theatres, including designing scenery and costumes as well as overseeing stage machinery at the Drury Lane Theatre managed by David Garrick and then by Richard Brinsley Sheridan from 1778. The Loutherbourg family would often come and stay at the Dumergues' for a few days, so that the whole clan – including the six Loutherbourg children, three of whom were of Sophia's and Charlotte's ages – would all go out and attend a play. Charlotte loved reading novels, but she had a particular fondness for plays, a passion that stemmed from her life experience with the Dumergues, especially since Charles Dumergue had shares in the Drury Lane Theatre.[170] At the beginning of Charlotte and Scott's married life, 'I doubt if they ever spent a week in Edinburgh without indulging themselves in this amusement'[171] – that is, watching plays – Lockhart wrote in his *Life of Sir Walter Scott*. Sutherland added: 'At this period, under his wife's cosmopolitan influence, he seems to have seen that career as one which would draw him to London and the Drury Lane stage.'[172]

This international creative circle became Charlotte's own social network, with few members later integrating into what I would call her husband's 'artistic coterie'. As described by Betty A. Schellenberg, though her book focused on literary coteries, a coterie is a 'select group of individuals linked by ties of friendship founded upon, or deepened by, mutual encouragement to original composition'.[173] In this case, it refers to original artistic composition, as Charlotte's cosmopolitan circle was more artistic than literary. I would definitely include Charlotte's London-

---

[167] Boulton was said to be one of Charles Dumergue's most esteemed friends. Charlotte was a favourite of his and is often mentioned in his papers. The Boulton papers have been carefully preserved at the Birmingham Archives, and among them are no fewer than one hundred letters to him from Dumergue and Sarah Nicolson.
[168] 'Letters chiefly of Sir Walter Scott, 1792–1817'. [169] Beauchamp, 2012: 3.
[170] Beauchamp, 2012: 3. [171] Lockhart, 1837–1838: 287. [172] Sutherland, 1995: 70.
[173] Schellenberg, 2016: 2.

based friends, English actor Daniel Terry and his wife, Scottish painter and interior designer Elizabeth Wemyss Nasmyth, in Scott's exclusive set of close artistic acquaintances. While Daniel Terry oversaw the building of the Scotts' home at Abbotsford with Scott, Elizabeth Nasmyth, born into the distinguished Nasmyth family of painters and art teachers, helped Charlotte decorate the house, particularly the Chinese drawing room. She painted much of the glass at Abbotsford and also produced designs for Scott's armoury. In exchange, and encouraged by Charlotte to write plays and adapt novels for the stage, Scott collaborated with Terry, seeking his literary advice on playwriting and entrusting him with stage adaptations of his works, including his late play *The Doom of the Devorgoil* (1830). There was a high level of trust and respect between the two men, with Terry even taking a financial stake in Scott's printing and publishing business with the Ballantynes, while Scott lent him money for his theatrical speculations.

Halfway through a journey whose destiny, unknown at the time, was to take her from France to Scotland, Charlotte transitioned from being distinctly French to embracing a new transcultural identity. Her artistic friends became part of Scott's social circle, with some even, I would argue, joining his 'artistic coterie'. Of course, as will be seen in Section 4, Scott also had a literary coterie of his own, exchanging manuscript materials with contemporary writers like Lady Morgan, Maria Edgeworth, and James Hogg, to name but a few, all of whom were published by the same publishers and translated by the same translators as Scott. His coterie was a select literary circle that Charlotte assisted, acting as his creative supporter and literary assistant. I am going to show that she contributed to Scott's literary production as an organiser of social literary gatherings, a secretary, a scribe, and a proofreader – nurturing a creative environment in a more behind-the-scenes, humble capacity. This explains why her role has remained so difficult to pinpoint and therefore largely understated to this day.

4 Transcultural Charlotte: Walter Scott's Creative Supporter and Literary Assistant

When lifting the veil of indifference, prejudice, or jealousy surrounding her, Charlotte Charpentier appears radically different from the way a few of her contemporaries and Scott's biographers have portrayed her. Far from being 'nearly an idiot'[174] who 'had no sympathy or appreciation of her husband's genius and literary work',[175] she stood at the centre of a circle of women who humbly supported Scott, helping him become a worldwide bestselling author.

---

[174] *Henry Fox Journal*, 1822: xx
[175] MacNalty, 1969: 35. See also 'She was shallow, ignorant, extravagant, pleasure-loving and thoroughly selfish,' Carswell, 1930: 27.

Figure 8 'Sir David Wilkie, 'The Abbotsford family', National Galleries of Scotland. Purchased 1895 and transferred from the National Gallery of Scotland 1936.

'The Abbotsford Family' (Figure 8), painted by David Wilkie in October 1817 and exhibited at the Royal Academy in 1818, powerfully and almost prophetically encapsulates the spirit of Scott's family literary business. It also demonstrates that art on such a celebrity scale required both artifice and teamwork. The artist artificially dressed the Scotts 'in the garb of South country peasants supposed to be concerting a merry-making'.[176] Charlotte and her daughters are grouped on the left, each holding a basket or pail of different sizes and uses as tokens of their collective labour. Her silhouette, in darker shades, stands out like an overshadowing presence at the back. She is singled out as the only woman wearing a hat and symbolically holding a set of keys in one hand, while the other, confounded with Anne's, seems to be pressing a pouch. She stands out against her daughters, who appear nearly conjoined. Sophia's arm encircles Anne's face, while the hems of their dresses align perfectly, and this is reinforced by the parallel positioning of their feet. Yet Sophia, drawn in the foreground and dressed in white and light pink, overshadows Anne and takes the limelight, foreshadowing her role as the guardian of Scott's afterlife.

---

[176] Walter Scott's letter to Adam Fergusson, 7 Mar. 1827.
www.walterscott.lib.ed.ac.uk/portraits/paintings/abbotfam.html.

4.1 Charlotte and the Castle-Building Foundation

The Scott business was a joint venture, a partnership between Scott and his wife. Charlotte Charpentier, Charlotte Scott from 1797, consistently supported him in all his endeavours, a commitment figuratively engraved in her title 'Lady Scott'. The capital letter 'L', with its prominent vertical line, graphically represents strength, stability, and upward progression. Its base, a solid foundation, suggests dependability and a grounding presence, aptly underscoring her role as a steadfast life companion: 'my Charlotte – my thirty years' companion', Scott wrote in his journal the day after her death in 1826, emphasising their close, unwavering bond.[177] Derived from Latin *companionem*, the noun 'companion' literally means 'bread fellow', reinforcing the title 'Lady', which refers to 'the one who kneads bread' (OED). Bread symbolises life and growth; here it represents literature – an intellectual nourishment and financial source of income they shared from their early courtship to her death, and almost beyond the grave. Scott felt unsettled about travelling to France without his late wife when in October 1826, he sought to complete research for his *Life of Napoleon Buonaparte*. He noted: 'This journey annoys me more than anything of the kind in my life. My wife's figure seems to stand before me and her voice is in my ears "S–, do not go – " It half frightens me. Strong throbbing at my heart and a disposition to be very sick.'[178] No wonder English portraitist James Saxon made a companion portrait of 'Lady Scott' in 1810 (Figure 9), following his 1805 portrait of her husband (Figure 10).

Charlotte was the chief backstage puppeteer, skilfully pulling the strings of the well-orchestrated décor of Abbotsford. Setting the scene and contributing tastefully to the décor under construction, she brought it to life with spirited conversations and musical interludes, thanks to her daughters Anne and Sophia playing the harp for their continuous flow of visitors of every class, both friends and strangers from near and far.[179] 'Visitors to the building site and imaginative play park of Abbotsford were desperate to visit the home of the Great Scott' – famously rumoured to be the anonymous author of the Waverley novels.[180] The statue of 'Morris begging for mercy from Helen MacGregor' in *Rob Roy*, located in the Sunken Garden, in the east courtyard, symbolises the blend of blank reality and fictitious romance surrounding him and his home. Visitors were 'seldom interested in his wife, perhaps because she could not inherit anything from the main attraction'.[181] She was seen merely as an imported

---

[177] Entry 16 May 1826; Anderson, 1972: 167.   [178] Entry 16 May 1826; Anderson, 1972: 240.

[179] 'I have the assurance of my sweet girl's taste in chusing whatever admits of decoration' (18 Nov. 1797) Scott confidently writes in his early correspondence to his bride-to-be; 'Letters chiefly of Sir Walter Scott, 1792–1817'.

[180] Archer-Thompson, 2018.   [181] Archer-Thompson, 2018.

Figure 9 James Saxon, 'Lady Scott', 1810. Abbotsford House, credit to the Faculty of Advocates Abbotsford Collection Trust.

Figure 10 James Saxon, 'Sir Walter Scott', 1771–1832. Novelist and poet. National Galleries of Scotland. Purchased 1904.

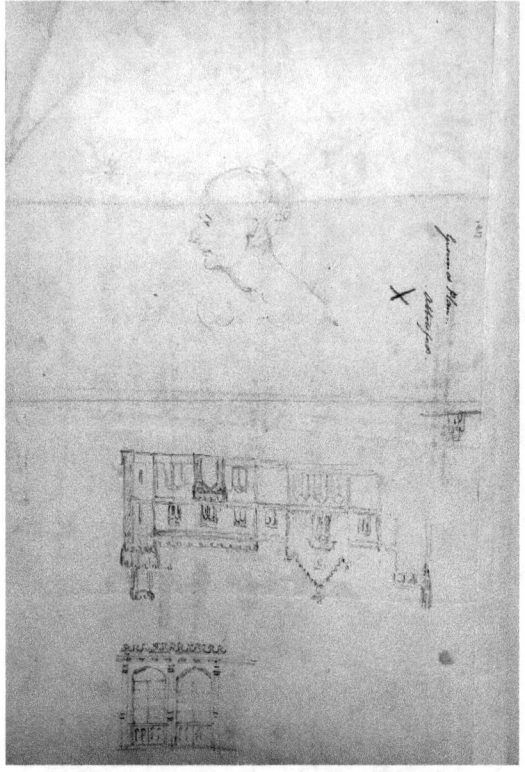

Figure 11 'Abbotsford Plans'. The Abbotsford Collection, credit to the Faculty of Advocates Abbotsford Collection Trust.

prop, even though she was actually part of the castle-building foundation, as shown by the architectural drawings for the proposed east extension of Abbotsford.

In the porfolio containing the house's plans in the Abbotsford Collection, there is a diptych-like loose sheet dated 1817 (Figure 11), with a pencilled sketch of a middle-aged woman in profile on one half, and ornate drawings of the house-to-be, with their sophisticated arabesques, on the other.[182] These artistic drawings sharply contrast with the geometric rigour of the other conventional architectural plans kept in the binder. 'An architect's doodles undoubtedly, but a tantalising glimpse of the Lady of the house and the wife of a patron, a powerful reminder that Abbotsford was her home to shape too', Archer-Thompson suggests.[183]

---

[182] 'Abbotsford Plans', Abbotsford Collection: 41.   [183] Archer-Thompson, 2018.

4.2 Charlotte's French Influence

Charlotte was an overshadowing and influential presence at Abbotsford, bestowing it with a French touch. She continued the practice – started in their summer house at Lasswade – of using the drawing room for more private occasions, not just for company as was the custom in Scotland.[184] The crockery was composed of French China that had been dispatched by waggon at the time of their settling in Edinburgh. 'I shall I believe send in the course of a fortnight a box of mine, that is if you will <u>give me leave</u>. It is a tea set, of french China, those sorts of goods could not conviniently travel with us, they can only go by the waggon'.[185] She vetoed some traditional Scottish dishes, so there was no serving of sheep's head or haggis in their house. 'She drew the line at these by no means ornamental disches,' Helen Russell reported in her *Personal History and Associations of Sir Walter Scott*.[186] And the meals were very transcultural, as attested by Scott alluding in French to a Scottish proverb, when hosting French critic and translator Amédée Pichot in August 1822: '"Nous vous donnons un déjeuner écossais, docteur, vous connaissez le proverbe: – Déjeuner écossais, dîner français, souper anglais."'[187]

At home, the Scotts lived in a relatively French linguistic environment, with all the children 'talk[ing] a little French under their mother's instruction'.[188] When travelling to France in 1815, Scott was agreeably surprised 'at the discovery that he could talk French fairly fluently; Charlotte deserved considerable credit for this'.[189] And his fluency in French was confirmed by Pichot when, in his travel diary, he quoted Scott's witty repartee given in French.[190] In fact, she had proposed to teach him French from the early days of their relationship: 'Adieu my dearest friend, étudiez votre français, I have a French Grammar for you,' she wrote.[191] It is yet another bilingual French grammar book that Scott had in his library study – where he preferred to keep reference books such as dictionaries, manuals, and practical books for his immediate needs – and that is still part of the Abbotsford Collection. It is Surenne's *Practical Grammar or French Rhetoric* that the author himself, Gabriel Jacques Surenne (1777–1858), had given to

---

[184] 'The landlady had called unexpectedly one morning, and was shocked to find her sitting alone in the drawing-room. Charlotte thought this was funny and told her mother-in-law about it, only to discover that the elder Mrs. Scott agreed with the landlady – a drawing-room was to be used for company only,' Dexter, 1960: 21.

[185] 23 Nov. 1797, 'Letters chiefly of Sir Walter Scott, 1792–1817'. The underlining, as well as typographical and grammatical errors, are as in the original.

[186] Russell, *Personal History and Associations of Sir Walter Scott*: 43.

[187] Pichot, 1825: 287–288.

[188] Letter to Lady Abercorn, 15 Mar. 1807, Grierson, 1937–1938: I:362.

[189] Dexter, 1960: 72.

[190] 'Cette saillie prouverait au besoin que sir Walter Scott connaît *assez bien* le français,' Pichot, 1825: 296.

[191] 2 Dec. 1797, 'Letters chiefly of Sir Walter Scott, 1792–1817'.

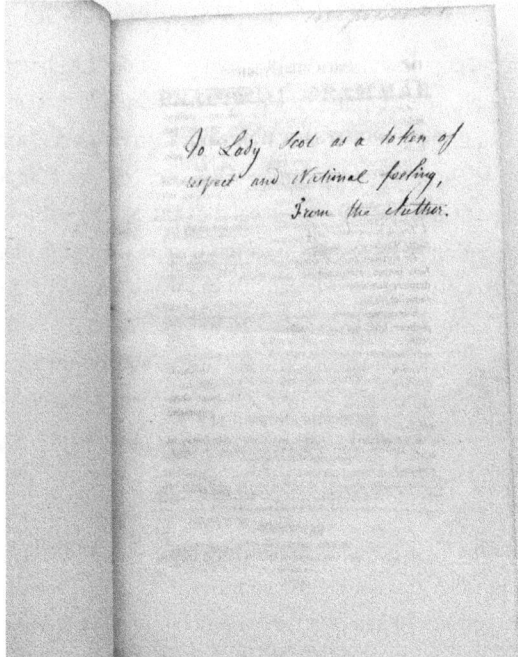

Figure 12 Surenne's *Practical Grammar or French Rhetoric*. Credit to the Faculty of Advocates Abbotsford Collection Trust. Abbotsford Library Study.

Charlotte: 'To Lady Scot as a token of respect and National feeling, from the Author' (Figure 12).

This personalised inscription to Charlotte can be explained by the affinity between the two French émigrés, both of whom had transformed and reinvented themselves after crossing the border. Now Edinburgh's leading French teacher and a prolific author of French educational textbooks, Surenne was originally a French-born military historian from near Paris who had emigrated to London, specifically Piccadilly – a neighbourhood Charlotte knew well from her time with the Dumergues – before settling in Edinburgh around 1816. At the top right-hand side of the page dedicated to Charlotte, there is an inscription, 'to be preserved', pencilled in Scott's handwriting. This was the label he used to mark the books he wished to keep at the time of his bankruptcy in 1826, when he was forced to part with many of his possessions. The book had been dear to them, as they had it personally bound (Figure 13) and stamped (Figure 14) with Scott's emblem, the portcullis – in honour of Abbotsford's portcullis gate – and the Latin motto 'Clausus Tutus Ero' ('Closed in I am safe').[192] Page 198 had been

---

[192] Scott explained the meaning of this 'mark of appropriation' in a letter to John Murray. See letter to Murray, 7 Feb. 1809, in Grierson, 1937–1938: II:168–169.

Figures 13 and 14 The cover and spine of Surenne's *Practical Grammar or French Rhetoric*. Credit to the Faculty of Advocates, Abbotsford Collection Trust.

earmarked, a section focused on orthology and grammatical construction, aiming to teach the elegance of expression and eloquence.

The Scotts' home was pervaded with French, which tended to permeate the English language, creating a continuum between languages. This partly explains why Scott would sprinkle his texts with French, Italian, or German at will.

Charlotte's written and spoken English was riddled with lexical and grammatical mistakes typical of a French native. 'A French accent – what Walter called a very slight foreign tinge in her pronunciation – stayed with her all her life, and in 1797 her writing showed a similar difficulty.'[193] Her English was interwoven with French through linguistic transfers, as demonstrated in the few preserved letters from 1797, particularly the two selected here to illustrate this point.[194] Her interferences between English and French could be phonetic: 'were' instead of 'where' ('he had a place under government, their residence

---

[193] Dexter, 1960: 5. [194] I have inserted asterisks to point out her mistakes.

was at Lyons, were* you would find on inquiries, that they lived in good repute', 25 Oct.), false cognates such as 'loose' and 'lose' ('I very soon after had the affliction of loosing* my mother,' 25 Oct.) or linked to her excessive use of the /h/ sound: 'Lord Downshire will be happy to hear from you, write soon has* he may be call'd away much sooner than he expect*, he is the very best man on hearth*' (7 Oct.). Like in this last example, her phonetic mistakes could be combined with morphosyntactic ones, such as incorrect verb agreements ('we should be educated, and even christen* to the church of England,' 25 Oct.), indiscriminate use of plurals, and irregular verb forms ('to prevent any little difficulties that might have arrisened*,' 25 Oct.). Her written English improved significantly from 1797 onward, but having lived among émigrés with the Dumergues in London, she never fully mastered it.

Scotland's long-standing relationship with France meant that French works – typically by Montesquieu, Rousseau, and, to a lesser extent, Voltaire – were translated into English and read in Scotland. Additionally, Lesage's *Gil Blas* and *Le Diable boîteux*, Fénelon's *Télémaque*, as well as his fables and dialogues, and Molière's plays were also widely read in the early nineteenth century.[195] Through Charlotte's influence, the Scotts' library included French books that differed from the popular ones commonly read in Scotland, including those just mentioned. Scott's remark to Charlotte in a letter from London on the eve of a still secret change of government suggests she was an avid reader: 'There's a turn for you – match it in your novels if you can.'[196] She 'kept in touch with French literature',[197] and Lindsay Levy's ten-year cataloguing of the Abbotsford library shows that the Scotts owned many books in French.[198] Some were held in both French and English, such as works by Rabelais and Montesquieu, along with an English version of Hugo's *Hernani*. These were the ones that Scott would also read. Their French collection included literature ranging from works by Mme de Staël to epistolary fiction such as *Lettres à Claire* by Mlle M.-L. Offroy de Barancy, as well as romance and erotic literature, like *Amours des dames and histoire amoureuse des Gaules* by comte de Bussy, *Les aventures du Baron de Foeneste* by Theodore Agrippa d'Aubigné, *L'heureux esclave* by Gabriel de Brémond, *Les amans heureux* by Thomas Catlett, or *Les Étrennes de la Saint-Jean* by comte de Caylus. Charlotte seems to have been particularly fond of Louvet de Couvray's libertine novels with their fast-paced romance, multiple twists, and comedic scenes. In addition to *Émilie de Varment: ou le divorce nécessaire, et les amours du Curé Sévin*, she owned

---

[195] To know more, see Marshall, 1978.
[196] 'James Glen Memorial' Collection, Notes, doc. 164, MS.S.2533. [197] Dexter, 1960: 75.
[198] Online catalogue of the Advocates and Abbotsford Libraries: https://advocates.ent.sirsidynix.net.uk/client/en_GB/abbotsford.

the three volumes of *Les Amours du chevalier de Faublas*. When in London, she had most likely seen Kemble and Storace's adaptation played at the Drury Lane Theatre in June 1794. Her bookcase also included French erotic poetry and fables, such as those published by Étienne Barbazan. Due to Charlotte's formidable fondness for plays, her book collection was remarkably rich in French drama. It featured classical works by Molière, Racine, and Le Sage, as well as anthologies like *Répertoire du théâtre françois* by Claude-Bernard Petitot.

4.3 Charlotte's Literary Hospitality

Charlotte was a great hostess, as 'incurably hospitable' as her husband, likely due to her past transcultural and sociable experiences in both Lyon and London.[199]

> The open-house hospitality which all commentators note as a feature of Abbotsford began with Charlotte's regime at 50 George Street.
>
> One of the very few facts which we know about the Charpentier household in Lyons where she was brought up was that many interesting strangers seem to have dropped in. So too did people drop in on the Scotts in the New Town and at the houses they later kept in the country.[200]

She seemed particularly keen to host her own countrymen and women, as evinced by Scott saying '"lady Scott sera bien aise de vous voir,"' when, in August 1822, they hosted anglophile Amédée Pichot.[201] This transcultural mediator was the first to translate Scott's poetry into French, including *The Lady of the Lake*, a copy of which he gave to Scott. The latter assured him it would give special pleasure to Lady Scott ('Je l'accepterai avec reconnaissance: elle fera plaisir à lady Scott. Vous me permettrez de vous présenter à elle').[202] Charlotte indeed extended the invitation to Abbotsford before hosting Pichot again at Castle Street, Edinburgh, during the festivities surrounding King George IV's visit, providing him with a ticket for a vantage-point seat.[203]

The French translator's visit was also the occasion for a transnational literary Scottish breakfast orchestrated by the Scotts and attended by English poet

---

[199] Expression used in Dexter's (1960) unpublished thesis, 'Sir Walter Scott and His Wife'. Despite their buoyant and generous hospitality, both Charlotte and Scott often complained that their homes, whether at Lasswade (1798–1804), Ashiestiel from 1804, or Abbotsford, were always full of guests who joined the family for every meal and often stayed for a few days at a time. In a letter to their former governess, Miss Millar, Sophia wrote that 'Mamma is quite tired of people, as we have never been alone all the summer' (4 Nov. 1820), while Scott sighed in private that his time was 'picked away by teaspoonfuls'. He did not preside formally at dinner, leaving his family in charge, but took whichever chair was left available when he came in from working in his study.

[200] Sutherland, 1995: 69.   [201] Pichot, 1825: 281.   [202] Pichot, 1825: 249.

[203] Pichot, 1825: 302.

George Crabbe. The conversation, transcribed by Pichot in his travel narrative, proves that Charlotte was actively engaging in the literary discussions at home and that she was well read and astute. On that point, Dexter mentioned:

> an undated note from her [Charlotte] to Chambers's Lending Library listing several women novelists (such as Mrs Inchbald and Miss Edgeworth) a selection of whose books she wished sent to Abbotsford. Her reading did not stop there. She enjoyed Crabbe, and he and other literary guests, both writers and publishers, presented her with volumes of their own production, for which they begged the honor of a place in her own bookcase.[204]

Though certainly not a writer herself, Charlotte was fully aware of the power of the written word – 'the *written word* holds authority until a writer finally arrives to refute his predecessor; but sometimes a quarter of a century passes between one book and the next', she remarked.[205] Thus she understood the responsibility that writers have due to their influential role in society. Here is the exchange as reproduced by Pichot:

> Lady Scott. '–Pour un Français, votre ami n'a pas été très galant envers les dames d'Écosse.'
> '–Si cela est, il en sera au désespoir; car il aime les dames de tous les pays, mais peut-être davantage celles d'Écosse.'
> Lady Scott. '–Mais où a-t-il vu qu'elles allaient nu-pieds?'
> M. Crabbe. '–Mais a-t-il dit cela?'
> J'exprimais le même doute par la même question.
> Lady Scott. '–Oui, oui, dans sa lettre sur Glasgow. Les Parisiennes ont dû bien rire aux dépens des sauvages beautés calédoniennes. Mais la perfidie, c'est d'avoir feint de chercher querelle aux petits pieds des Françaises. M. Nodier ou ses compagnons de voyage ont-ils réellement vu des dames en Écosse courir pieds nus ? ... On n'est pas galant quand on voit les dames d'Écosse courir pieds nus.'[206]

In this quoted literary exchange with Crabbe, Pichot, and her husband, Charlotte teasingly shared her views on the work of Dr Johnson, a 'very demanding man' who 'did not come here as a friend. His account did not tend to dissipate the prejudices of his compatriots in regard to Scotland. He was a bad-tempered writer', she provocatively declared, with a value judgement apparently lacking literary depth and critical distance.[207] Apparently only because Charlotte was very spiritual, taking everything with a pinch of salt, as proved by her 1797 courtship letters to Scott where she feigned indifference and even anger towards her husband-to-be. Here, through her seemingly frivolous comment, she crisply emphasised Samuel Johnson's objective, which was to capture the last records of

---

[204] Dexter 1960: 74–75.   [205] My translation, Pichot, 1825: 291.
[206] Pichot, 1825: 293–296.   [207] Pichot, 1825: 289.

a primitive and wild Scotland, thereby demonstrating her familiarity with his *Journey to the Western Islands of Scotland*. She similarly criticised Charles Nodier's *Promenade de Dieppe aux montagnes d'Écosse* for his prejudiced portrayal of Scottish women as wild, barefoot savages. She even proved her superior knowledge of his work by quoting a reference from chapter 15 on Glasgow that none of the literary men around her remembered.[208] She skilfully countered her three interlocutors, including her husband who had just praised Nodier's poetic style (p. 292), by purposely focusing on an apparently trivial detail and making it the book's central argument, thus curtailing the discussion. With a double rhetorical flourish, she ironically highlighted that both Glaswegian and Parisian women were being disparaged by Pichot's friend.

This extract from Pichot's memoir is just one testimony of Charlotte's deep interest in literature and her active engagement with it. The practice of literary exchanges was central to their relationship from the start, as evidenced by their 1797 courtship letters. On 18 November 1797, Scott wrote Charlotte a letter quoting a passage from Sheridan's comedy *The Rivals* (1775) without naming it: 'You know to Sheridan's peasant "thro winters'chilling woes,/ is all the warmth this little cottage knows."'[209] He knew she would recognise it, especially since she was familiar with the Irish playwright who then owned the Theatre Royal, Drury Lane. They flirted by exchanging familiar literary references, creating a special bond. In the month before, Scott had described his evenings 'spent in translating little tales from the German, which perhaps may serve poor passetemps, when I have my lovely friend to read them to'.[210] He had dreamt of reading literature to his wife, and this literary sharing continued throughout their lives. In a letter from 1813 to his friend American writer and diplomat Washington Irving, Scott similarly recounted that he had 'employed these few evenings in reading them [referring to the sketches from Irving's 1809 literary parody *History of New York*] aloud to Mrs S. and two ladies who are our guests, and our sides have been absolutely sore with laughing'.[211]

In addition to reading literature aloud, the Scotts would exchange literary gifts. In the Abbotsford Library Collection, there is a translation into English from the German of Gottfried August Bürger's *Leonora* (1796) that Scott gave

---

[208] 'Presque toutes les femmes de la classe intermédiaire, et un assez grand nombre de femmes de la classe élevée, marchent à pieds nus. Quelques unes ont adopté les souliers seulement. Les dames à la mode, qui ont emprunté les vêtements des Parisiennes, ont aussi emprunté leur chaussure, ou plutôt la nôtre; car elles sont chaussées en hommes: mais cette partie de leur accoutrement est celle qui les incommode le plus, et dont elles se défont le plus volontiers quand elle sont libres,' Nodier, 1821: 161.
[209] Oct. 1797, 'Letters chiefly of Sir Walter Scott, 1792–1817'.
[210] 23 Apr. 1813, 'Letters chiefly of Sir Walter Scott, 1792–1817'. [211] Irving, 1862: 240.

Figure 15 Charlotte's name on the inside page of *Leonora*. Abbotsford Library, credit to the Faculty of Advocates, Abbotsford Collection Trust.

to his wife just after their wedding. Scott had inscribed Charlotte's name in ink on the inside page (Figure 15).

Yet this English translation was not his translation of Bürger's ballad, which was published the same year as his translation of Bürger's *William and Helen*. Scott had improvised as a translator of German after just six weeks of study, and his translations of Bürger's works, as well as Goethe's *Götz von Berlichingen* (1799) three years later, were rather poor. Instead, he gave Charlotte a bilingual English–German edition translated by William Robert Spencer, featuring beautiful illustrations by Lady Diana Beauclerck, an English noblewoman and celebrated artist. Spencer, an English poet whom Scott warmly praised, was related to the illustrator – Lady Diana Beauclerk was his aunt on his father's side. Through this gift to Charlotte, Scott also indirectly encouraged family artistic collaboration.

4.4 Charlotte's Creative Assistance in Scott's Literary Process

Charlotte's role in shaping part of Scott's celebrity extended beyond being a gracious hostess and grand mistress of ceremonies. Indeed, she managed all aspects, human and material, of the domestic circle – family and guests, as well as garden and interior design – so it is hardly surprising that the completion of Abbotsford, Scott's financial ruin, and her own death nearly coincided.

Yet, as was often the case with the wives of great men, her role extended beyond the typical narrative that confined women to blissful domesticity and perpetuated 'the romantic myth of the "man of letters" as a solitary genius'.[212] In truth, as this subsection will demonstrate, she inspired him and actively assisted him in his literary endeavours, acting as his secretary, copyist, and proofreader. She was one of Scott's key assistants, serving as a bridge between his social networks and literary coterie.

4.4.1 Charlotte as Scott's Influential Support in His Work

Charlotte was omnipresent in his work – though between the lines – serving as her husband's main source of inspiration, his creative catalyst, and the driver of his imagination. 'Scott had the habit of taking traits or circumstances which he had met in real life and putting them into a novel in quite a different setting,' Dexter stated, and he progressively drew more and more from his wife's epic experience.[213] Her life had been eminently eventful, supplying Scott with rich material for his novels, with its share of mystery regarding her origins and her transnational journey from one social and linguistic milieu to another. Initially, in the poems the associations were vague and subtle, suggesting her influence without explicitly stating it. In *The Lay of the Last Minstrel* (1805), the heroine is named Margaret, Charlotte's first name, and the poem contains two beautiful apostrophes to love, particularly in Canto V. This section illustrates Scott's vision of a durable relationship, not based on a hot fiery passion, which is often short-lived, but on a true sympathetic bond:

> True love's the gift that God has given
> To man alone beneath the heaven.
> It is not Fantasy's hot fire,
> Whose wishes, soon as granted, fly;
> It liveth not with fierce desire,
> With dead desire it doth not die;
> It is the secret sympathy,
> The silver cord, the silken tie,
> Which heart to heart, and mind to mind,
> In body and in soul can bind.[214]

This stanza contrasts fleeting, impulsive emotions ('fantasy', 'fierce desire') with the enduring, balanced nature of true love, grounded in the importance of the mind. It culminates in the final couplet with the phrase 'mind to mind', which

---

[212] Sabiron, 2017: 61, 62.   [213] Dexter, 1960: 95.   [214] Scott, [1805]: 139.

mirrors itself and elevates the role of thought, understanding, and rational connection. The strong internal rhythm and regular AABBCC rhyme scheme reflect harmony and intellectual equality – especially in the rhyme between 'mind' and 'bind'. The stanza also evokes delicate, almost invisible bonds through the lexical field of subtlety ('secret sympathy', 'silver cord', 'silken tie'), suggesting that the most profound connections are intangible and refined, like that between Scott and Charlotte, whose influence deepened as he began writing his novels. His Waverley protagonists – such as Edward Waverley or Frank Osbaldistone in *Rob Roy* (1817) – undertake a transnational northward journey, central to the plot and modelled on Charlotte's own personal trajectory from Lyon to Paris in France, then to London in England, and finally to Scotland.

In addition to travelling northward, the typical Scott hero is an orphan going through adventures, reflecting the theme of resilience and personal growth inspired by Charlotte's early upbringing. Edward Waverley is raised by his uncle Sir Everard Waverley after his father's absence; Wilfred of Ivanhoe is effectively estranged from his father, Cedric of Rotherwood, and must make his way in the world largely on his own. Though not an orphan in the traditional sense, Lucy Ashton from *The Bride of Lammermoor* (1819) suffers from the absence of parental protection and guidance, leading to her tragic fate. Similarly, Jeanie Deans and her sister, Effie, from *The Heart of Midlothian* (1818) face significant familial and societal challenges without substantial parental support, while Harry Bertram from *Guy Mannering* (1815) is separated from his family, effectively orphaned by circumstance.

Charlotte's physical appearance and character are often represented through the pairs of contrasting female protagonists that feature in Scott's novels. Scott attributes Charlotte's traits and qualities to each of them, without any being directly modelled after her: Rose Bradwardine and Flora Mac-Ivor in *Waverley* (1814), Diana Vernon and Helen MacGregor in *Rob Roy*, Rowena and Rebecca in *Ivanhoe* (1819), Lucy Ashton and Alice Gray in *The Bride of Lammermoor*. The heroine who is most closely modelled after Charlotte is Julia Mannering, the daughter of the eponymous protagonist in *Guy Mannering*. Through Scott's letters and the testimonies of family friends, Charlotte was described as small, graceful, and pretty, though 'not a beauty by any means', Scott added in his letter to his aunt.[215] However, he was not given to bragging, and no doubt he also wanted to preempt any criticism from his family, who might not have found her pretty enough. In *Guy Mannering*, Julia is said to be 'of the middle size, or rather less, but formed with much elegance; piercing dark eyes, and jet-black

---

[215] 'She is not a beauty by any means, but her person and face are engaging – she is a brunette.' Letter to Miss Rutherford, late Oct. 1797, Grierson, 1937–1938: I:76.

hair of great length, corresponded with the vivacity and intelligence of features, in which were blended a little haughtiness, and a little bashfulness, a great deal of shrewdness, and some power of humorous sarcasm'.[216] Like Charlotte who suffered from the 'uncommon cold weather ... in the north climate'[217] when first settling in Scotland, Julia was 'furred and mantled up to the throat against the severity of the weather'.[218]

Yet the Scott protagonist, though not female, whose situation most closely resembles Charlotte's is Darsie Latimer from *Redgauntlet* published in 1824. His very name is a concentration of references pointing to France and to Charlotte's transcultural status. Darsie is a variation on the gender-neutral French name Darcy, which was first used as a nickname for someone with dark hair and appeared in Normandy in the Middle Ages, while his surname, Latimer, comes from the Old French 'latinier' or 'latimier', derived from Latin 'latimarius', meaning 'interpreter' or 'translator', clearly defining him as a mediator of language and culture. Darsie is portrayed as a young man of uncertain parentage who has been transplanted from England to Edinburgh in childhood and whose surname, like Charlotte's, was given to him when he arrived in Scotland. 'I ask you ... whether you can remember that you were ever called Latimer, until you had that name given you in Scotland'.[219] 'I am alone in the world; my only guardian writes to me of a large fortune which will be mine when I reach the age of twenty-five complete,' Darsie writes in his journal to his inseparable friend and protector Alan Fairford.[220] The latter, with his reliable, supportive and reasonable nature, is a blend of Walter Scott – Fairford is a young, upright advocate like him – and Charlotte's guardian, Arthur Hill, the Marquess of Downshire, whose initial title as a young man was Lord Fairford. In a letter to Alan, Darsie wrote that his friend's father, a striking portrait of Scott's own father, who was reluctant for his son to marry someone with no origin,

> quarrels a little – I will not say with my want of ancestry, but with my want of connexions. He reckons me a lone thing in this world, Alan, and so, in good truth I am; and it seems a reason to him why you should not attach yourself to me, that I can claim no interest in the general herd. .... In a country where all the world have a circle of consanguinity, extending to their cousins at least, I am a solitary individual, having only one kind heart to throb in unison with my own.[221]

It is a well-developed characterisation, not only distantly inspired by but closely and fully modelled on Charlotte.

---

[216] Scott, [1815] (1999): 106–107.
[217] Letter from Charlotte Carpenter to Lord Downshire, 26 Nov. 1797, in 'Letters chiefly of Sir Walter Scott, 1792–1817'.
[218] Scott, [1815] (1999): 107. [219] Scott, [1824] (1997): 171. [220] Scott, [1824] (1997): 1.
[221] Scott, [1824] (1997): 3, 4.

Over time, Scott's literary production grew increasingly inspired by her, so that with her death in 1826, it felt as if he could no longer benefit from her inspirational influence and draw from her life to nourish his literary imagination. From then on, Scott was unable to transform her romanesque life into fiction without her presence. A few years before her death when her health was declining, Scott resumed writing plays, a genre he had been involved with at the beginning of his career, mostly through Charlotte's incentive. Scott's last works were mostly French-focused but left the novelistic – apart from *Count Robert of Paris* (1832) – to verge purely towards the historical and factual. His voluminous *Life of Napoleon Buonaparte, Emperor of the French* was published in 1827 and represented an important contribution to the study of France during the Napoleonic era, while his *Tales of a Grandfather: The History of France*, aiming at a younger audience, was left unfinished in 1831.

Everything is closely intertwined in Scott's life, both family and literary endeavours: 'The period of Scott's search for a wife (1794–1797) coincides with his first serious attempts at authorship,' so that the loss of his wife also coincides with his financial ruin and the relative failure of his literary imagination.[222]

4.4.2 Charlotte's Role as Mediator and Amanuensis to Scott

Scott was 'a man who approached all venues of creative process with a collaborative bent, from storytelling to home building', but the concept of 'social authorship' alone cannot explain Scott's writing process and Charlotte's role in it.[223] Social authorship, as thoroughly explored in Margaret J. M. Ezell's 1999 book *Social Authorship and the Advent of Print*, refers to the '"game" of authorship' at play 'in the period in which print was becoming the dominant, conventional mode of transmitting what we consider literary and academic writing but also during which manuscript circulation was still a viable and competitive technology'.[224] This practice was particularly common from the 1680s to the 1790s. Even though Scott, as noted by many scholars – including Ina Ferris (2012) in 'Scott's Authorship and Book Culture' – engaged with the concept of social authorship, it was often more of an ironic stance. This is metafictionally illustrated at the outset of *The Bride of Lammermoor* (1819) through the metaphor of the womblike writing laboratory in the fictitious village of 'Gandercleugh' (from Scots, meaning 'a goose basin'), underscoring the playful nature of his authorial identity.[225] This name humorously suggests a retreat where the storyteller, his assistant, and his scribe, darken the paper

---

[222] Sutherland, 1995: 64.   [223] Archer-Thompson, 2018.   [224] Ezell, 1999: 1.
[225] I have made a more lengthy metafictional micro-reading of this passage in my chapter, Sabiron, 2017: 62.

with a quill pen made from a goose feather. In this novel, Scott invites readers to embark on a literary scavenger hunt involving riddles and guessing names: Jedidiah Cleishbotham supposedly collects and arranges tales written by his schoolhouse assistant, Peter Pattieson, from stories recounted by the unnamed Landlord of the Wallace Arms. But decoding the conundrum, the latter's initials 'WA' strikingly mirror those of the anonymous Author of Waverley, 'AW' – that is, Walter Scott. The invented, pun-filled, fictitious storyteller Jedidiah Cleishbotham is one of Scott's pseudonyms, showcasing his playful use of masks.[226] Through anamorphosis, however, it can also be Charlotte in disguise, as 'Jedidiah' is a biblical name meaning 'beloved of the Lord'. With a light-hearted twist, she is figuratively characterised as 'beating the bottom' ('Cleishbotham') which humorously underlines the significant part she played in assisting Scott in his literary business. In a letter from 10 December 1824 to Mrs Marianne Clephane, Scott claimed in jest that his wife chastised him while he wrote for not making an invitation 'half pressing enough'.[227] Charlotte's alleged authoritative nature was a running joke between them. This metafictional, playful parody of social authorship demonstrates that Scott surrounded himself with numerous individuals who nurtured his creativity and influenced his writing, even though the final work was ultimately the solitary effort of a single author, especially after his writing of *The Minstrelsy of the Scottish Border* (1802). This anthology of border ballads, alongside some modern literary ones, was probably more of a joint effort, drawing from traditional tales steeped in the spirit of the frontier, as recounted by Scott's grandmother, Barbara Scott, his favorite aunt, Jeanie, and an old servant, Alison Wilson – who were wonderful storytellers.[228] For this first work, Scott had also enlisted the help of fellow Scotsmen James Hogg, William Laidlaw, and especially John Leyden – a scholar of extraordinary ability who practically lived at the Scotts' house – as well as two Englishmen: Richard Heber, a renowned book collector, and antiquary George Ellis, an authority on early English poems and romances.

Apart from this particular case early on in his career, however, Scott's model of a literary network was more akin to a coterie, a common type of writing network in early modern England. Scott's literary circle resembled a cohesive social community – a closed circle of readers and writers bound by 'strong shared literary interests, expressed in the scribal exchange of original compositions, reading materials and critical views'.[229] In Scott's literary coterie, there were

---

[226] Sabiron, 2017: 60.
[227] Letter to Mrs Clephane, 7 Dec. 1824, Grierson, 1937–1938: VIII:450.
[228] 'Correspondence, 1930–1935, of James Glen, Writer, Glasgow, chiefly with Professor Sir Herbert Grierson', James Glen's letter to Prof. Grierson, 29 Oct., Grierson, 1930: 16.
[229] Schellenberg, 2016: 9.

Archibald Constable and the Ballantynes (his publishers), as well as numerous antiquarians, book collectors, and writers with whom he corresponded a lot. The 'Millgate Union Catalogue of Walter Scott Correspondence' records more than fourteen thousand letters written by or to Scott.[230] Hence his culture of letter writing, which was 'not always a private exercise but a household responsibility, and the Scotts were undoubtedly working and communicating as a partnership'.[231] They had a tendency to either dictate or delegate writing, as Charlotte famously disliked doing it herself – a fact reflected in the following sentence, which typically blends a wishful tone with a more assertive one ('certainly', 'make') in its final, hypothetical ('would') main clause: 'I shall be very happy to hear from her [referring to Scott's mother], but cant say that of having to write, I wish you would do it for me, if that was possible, I certainly would make you do it' – a threat she carried out as soon as she was married.[232] 'I have not wrote to the Misses Pattinsons, it was only to be when I was settled in Edinburgh, then you are to be my Secretary, I will give you that appointment, it won't be a very profitable one.'[233] The capital 'S' in 'Secretary' reinforces the sense of order implied by the 'be + to + verb' structure ('are to be'), humorously suggesting a formal title, as Charlotte playfully reverses the roles ('my Secretary') – casting herself as the 'Author' and Scott as her 'Secretary'.

Her handing over the task of writing to her husband is confirmed by a letter from Joanna Baillie, whom Charlotte had most probably met in London through their shared love of theatre and their mutual scientific connections. Baillie was in London at the same time as Charlotte, having moved there in 1784 after the death of one of her uncles, William Hunter. He and his brother, John, both based in the English capital, were leading scientific figures of the eighteenth century. Baillie's brother, Matthew, also became a renowned physician among the London elite – like Charles Dumergue – treating King George III for his neurological disorders. Given their roles in caring for the royal couple and their mutual interest in theatre, it is likely that the Dumergues and the Baillies crossed paths. Joanna Baillie later became part of Scott's literary coterie, engaging in regular literary correspondence with him:

> If Mrs Scott has such a substitute as you to answer her letters, she must keep it a secret, else she will have letters from all corners of the country poured upon her, from ladies who will be glad to say, they have received a letter the

---

[230] https://digital.nls.uk/catalogues/walter-scott-correspondence.
[231] Archer-Thompson, 2018.
[232] 14 Nov. 1797, 'Letters chiefly of Sir Walter Scott, 1792–1817'. Underlining as in the original. See also 'Though you do not like to write you have had the goodness to say you are not displeased with receiving letters,' Oct. 1797, 'Letters chiefly of Sir Walter Scott, 1792–1817'.
[233] 23 Nov. 1797, 'Letters chiefly of Sir Walter Scott, 1792–1817'. The underlining, as well as typographical and grammatical errors, are as in the original.

other day from Walter Scott. ... Thanks to you then for your letter, whether it came to me from your own good will or Mrs Scott; and thank Mrs Scott for me for having so kindly put you upon the service.[234]

Baillie's playful writing humorously blurs the line between the personal pronouns 'you' and 'her' – the letter's sender and the secret substitute writing on her behalf.

Charlotte was one of the few people privy to the secret of Scott's authorship, which he only publicly revealed in 1827. 'The veil was kept [...] [on all] of Scott's family, except of course his wife,'[235] Lockhart recalled in his biography of Scott. She served as an essential 'bridge', or 'broker'[236] between the family, Scott's literary coterie and other networks, owing to his many concomitant occupations – sheriff depute of Selkirk from 1799, clerk to the Edinburgh Court of Session from 1806 and partner in the Ballantynes' printing firm from 1799, in addition to his prolific writing and other responsibilities, including hosting guests.

From the very beginning, Charlotte assisted Scott in his literary production by serving as one of his amanuenses. This began with *The Minstrelsy of the Scottish Border* (1802), for which Charlotte 'probably had no ballad lore to begin with'.[237] However, alongside Anne Ellis – who became a close friend after the Scotts and Ellises met in 1803 – she copied the collected border ballads, whether they were ultimately published or not. 'Both women were interested in their husbands' writing and were willing, skilful copyists.'[238] This role is evidenced by a letter John Leyden addressed to Richard Heber in November 1800 from Lasswade, mentioning Charlotte's difficulty in deciphering Heber's notoriously bad handwriting, which she then had to copy: 'Mrs Scott begs you will either procure a little better ink or allow her to send you a bottle of her own making, that everyone may not be obliged to sit gaping round Scott who swears every three words that your handwriting is little better to read than a Runic inscription or a weatherbeaten whinestone.'[239] Charlotte's assistance, kept secret even from her own children, is attested to by Scott's contemporary biographer George Allan:

> As will sometimes happen, however, the very indifference which Lady Scott testified respecting her husband's labours contributed to confirm many in the belief of her secretly assisting him; and, what will scarcely be credited, even her own family were of the number. Mr. Laidlaw told a friend of ours, that Miss Scott, (now Mrs Lockhart) who, whatever were her suspicions, was as really ignorant of the Waverley secret as the world was in general, once mentioned to him the circumstance of her mother's copy of the novels remaining so long uncut in her chamber, as confirming her belief, not only that her father was the author of them, but that her mother must be privy to the mystery,

---

[234] 2 Oct. 1808, 'Letters chiefly of Sir Walter Scott, 1792–1817'.
[235] Lockhart, 1837–1838: 201. [236] Schellenberg, 2016: 216. [237] Dexter, 1960: 32.
[238] Dexter, 1960: 38. [239] Heber and Cholmondeley, 1950: 175.

if not actually assisting in their compilation: arguing, that if she had not known every thing about them beforehand, she must have shared in the curiosity to peruse them, evinced by every body else, upon their publication.[240]

One of the ballads Charlotte copied was 'The Eve of St John', which was published in *The Minstrelsy of the Scottish Border*. Scott had written this imitation of ancient ballads for her in 1799. Her copy was written in an already existing notebook with an oxblood calf binding and gold tooling, as would have been typical for a gentry notebook of the time. It was made by a bookbinder or bookseller (Figure 16), with unused pages removed (Figure 17) before the entire book was presented as a gift to Scott's uncle, Captain Robert Scott of Rosebank (Figure 18). After his death in 1804, it was passed on to Scott's aunt, Barbara Scott. It is a tiny but astonishingly beautiful transcription, which Charlotte illustrated herself with a sepia watercolour of Smailholm Tower (Figure 19). This tower, the setting for the poem, held deep emotional significance for Scott, as he visited his paternal grandfather there as a boy. The booklet is entirely in Charlotte's hand, as evident when comparing her handwriting in letters to this script, and confirmed by James Hamilton, research principal at the Signet Library where the book is stored.[241]

Charlotte was a gifted artist who could draw very well, contrary to her husband. Scott often publicly regretted what he called his 'ignorance of drawings',[242] which he tried to overcome by taking lessons and putting in great effort, much like he did with music, but to no avail: "'I took lessons of oil-painting in youth. . . . But I could make no progress in either painting or drawing. Nature denied me the correctness of eye and neatness of hand. Yet I was very desirous to be a draughtsman at least – and laboured harder to attain that point than at any other in my recollection to which I did not make some approaches.'"[243] In the James Glen Memorial Collection, which includes the 'Letters of Sir Walter Scott' and his correspondence with Charlotte, there are border illustrations likely drawn by Charlotte (Figure 20).[244] These decorative marginalia seem to have served as drafts for embellishments in a medieval-themed manuscript. On top of traditional animals such as rabbits, fish, and toads, the illustrator added various fantastical and mythological creatures to the borders for decoration or to amuse the reader.

They could be connected to the supernatural aspects of 'The Lay of the Last Minstrel' (1805), Scott's narrative poem set in the mid sixteenth century, particularly the goblin Gilpin Horner. This local legend was woven into the work initially intended for the third volume of the *Minstrely of the Scottish Border*, following

---

[240] Allan, 1834: 485.

[241] Photos I have taken – apart from Figure 16 that was taken by James Hamilton, research principal at the Signet Library – when visiting the Signet Library in Edinburgh on 15 Apr. 2024.

[242] Lockhart, 1837–1838: 15.   [243] Lockhart, 1837–1838: 35.

[244] 'Letters chiefly of Sir Walter Scott, 1792–1817'.

Figure 16 The edge of the notebook used for 'The Eve of St John', reproduced with permission of the Signet Library

Figure 17 Already existing notebook, reproduced with permission of the Signet Library

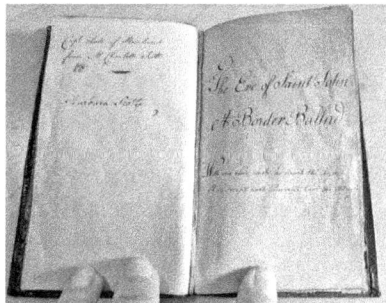

Figure 18 Inside pages of 'The Eve of St John' with dedications and title, reproduced with permission of the Signet Library.

Figure 19 Watercolour and title in a dramatic Gothicised script, reproduced with permission of the Signet Library.

Figure 20 Decorative marginalia likely drawn by Charlotte, reproduced under a Creative Commons Attribution 4.0 International (CC-BY) licence with the permission of the National Library of Scotland. https://creativecommons.org/licenses/by/4.0.

the suggestion of the Countess of Dalkeith, who had asked Scott to write a ballad based on an old legend of the Buccleugh family. Charlotte actually wrote a full transcript of the poem that her husband presented to Lady Dalkeith, along with an apology she had dictated: "'that the ornaments would have been better executed had it not been for the shortness of the days, which obliged the transcriber to work by candle light'". This anecdote was recounted by Dexter, who had been permitted by the Duke of Buccleugh to examine the transcript carefully. Impressed by the quality of Charlotte's artistic work, Dexter added 'The apology was unnecessary, – the work was beautifully done, and beside "ornaments" it had a number of excellent illustrations.'[245]

Charlotte indeed copied and illustrated many of her husband's poems for his literary correspondents, including numerous female friends such as Miss Carmichael and Lady Abercorn, as illustrated in his 1807 letters:[246]

> Mrs Scott is quite ashamed and sorry that she has not been able to furnish the transcript which she intends for your Ladyship's acceptance. The trifles it contains have been so long dispersed that she has found it very difficult matter to get copies of them from those into whose possession they had gone. She has now recovered all she thinks worth preserving and is busy with her copy. . . . I hope to bring up Mrs. Scott's Manuscript along with me & to have the honour of presenting it myself.[247]

Scott wrote to her on 31 January 1807. Lady Abercorn was a great admirer of his work and one of his closest correspondents, often offering feedback on his writing.

Yet Scott's remark underscored Charlotte was not merely an amanuensis rewriting what others – and Scott in particular – had drafted to create additional copies or to help conceal Scott's secret authorship, as was the case with Lady Abercorn who was not entrusted with the secret of his authorship until 1820. She also conducted her own research to find, as in this case, scattered fragments of the ballad, recollect the pieces and create a noteworthy whole. The very striking expression 'Mrs Scott's Manuscript' is highlighted in the middle of the sentence with the alliterations of /m/, /s/, and /t/ sounds, placing Scott in the position of grammatical object ('along with me', 'presenting it myself'). It is as if they had swapped roles, with the writer becoming the messenger and cultural mediator, and his wife and literary assistant becoming the fictitious writer of the *Ballad of Queen Orraca* ordered by Lady Abercorn.[248] In 1810, it is again to Mrs Scott that the latter appealed to have a copy of *The Lady of the Lake*: 'I am sure Mrs Scott who is always so good to me, would have written it for me. I am almost hurt at seeing an account of it in the Irish Paper the very day I receive your letter, for I consider myself one of your most confidential friends,' Lady Abercorn regretted to Scott.[249]

---

[245] Dexter, 1960: 43. See her note 2: 'The artistic work was much more finished and beautiful than I had anticipated.'
[246] Letter of Sir Walter Scott to Mrs Hamilton sending of copy of 'The Lay of the Last Minstrel' for Miss Carmichael.
[247] Letter to Lady Abercorn, 31 Jan. 1807, Grierson, 1937–1938: I:350–351.
[248] Letter to Lady Abercorn, 15 Mar. 1807, Grierson, 1937–1938: I:361.
[249] Partington, 1930: 138.

'In the days before typewriter and camera, it was no small advantage to have a copyist and artist in the house, and Charlotte was particularly skillful,'[250] Dexter underscored, with probably many examples of her work having disappeared, unmentioned. And Charlotte had a lot of copying to do: even though it is not widely known or acknowledged, Scott corresponded with a large circle of women who served as proofreaders and critics and, like Lady Abercorn, were not entrusted with the secret of his authorship for some years. Hence, in March 1803, Charlotte transcribed *Cadyow Castle* with illustrations for both Lady Anne Hamilton and English poet Anna Seward.[251] The following year, she copied 'The Lay of the the Last Minstrel' for amateur artist Lady Douglas.[252] Yet most of her transcriptions were for Scott's close friend Lady Abercorn. This included the first two cantos of *Marmion* sent in September 1807, followed by the entire historical romance three months later:

> I have defered writing from day to day my dear Lady Abercorn until I should be able to make good my promise of sending you the two first cantos of Marmion. ...
>
> I am also anxious to know how you like Marmion & whether the Marquis has seen it. I have some dread of his criticism as he understands the niceties of the English language better than anyone I ever met with.[253]

Charlotte's presence is pervasive, evident between the lines even when she is not directly mentioned by Scott as his amanuensis. However, copying was not her only task in assisting Scott; she also served as one of his proofreaders.

4.4.3 Charlotte's Role as Scott's Proofreader

Charlotte's apparent indifference to her husband's literary production was taken at face value by many commentators and critics of the time. This false assumption persisted over time, eventually being accepted as truth. Completely overlooked was the fact that she did not need to read her husband's work upon publication as she already knew it all, being involved in the secret of its fabrication.

Charlotte was Scott's first reader and literary confidante, as Scott acknowledged in his private journal: 'It withers my heart ... to recollect that I can hardly hope again to seek confidence and counsel from that ear to which all

---

[250] Dexter, 1960: 43.
[251] Letter to Anna Seward, 17 Oct. 1802, Grierson, 1937–1938: I:163, 'I am highly flatterd by your approbation of Cadyow Castle'; letter to Lady Abercorn, Mar. 1803, Grierson, 1937–1938: I:180.
[252] Letter of Sir Walter Scott to Lady Douglas, sending proofs of 'The Lay of the Last Minstrel'.
[253] Letter to Lady Abercorn, 10 Sept. 1807, Grierson, 1937–1938: I: 381; letter to Lady Abercorn, 21 Dec. 1807, Grierson, 1937–1938: I:406.

might be safely confided,' he feared.[254] This fear he gravely yielded to on the day after her demise: 'I am deprived of the sharer of my thoughts and counsels.'[255] Recognising her invaluable input through the possessive pronoun 'hers', Scott reflected on her deathbed, 'I wonder how I shall do with the large portion of thoughts which were hers for thirty years.'[256] He even likened his late wife to Tanneguy du Châtel, the fifteenth-century Breton knight and leading adviser to King Charles VII of France, using a fitting French phrase: 'Ballantyne thinks well of the work – very well – But I shall [expect] inaccuracies. And' it were to do again I would get some one to look it over. But who could that some one be? Whom is there left of human race that I could hold such close intimacy with? No one. *Tanneguy du Châtel, ou es-tu!*'[257] Through this rhetorical question, Scott twisted the reference to a note attached to the pall of Charles VII, with these words: '*Tanneguy du Chatel où es tu? Mais il etoit François*'.[258] Despite being disgraced and exiled to his estate after rendering great services, the first chamberlain had nevertheless hurried to court at his own expense to organise a funeral for his master, whose last rites had been neglected. Through this historical French reference, Scott highlighted Charlotte's devotion as his creative supporter and literary assistant.

Helen Russell of Ashiestiel, a relative of Scott on his mother's side, confirmed her assistance, going even further by mentioning Charlotte's visit to the Ballantynes' printing house:

> She certainly did read her husband's works in some form. It is not what one would have otherwise expected, but the daughters told Lockhart, when he first became intimate with the family, that one of the reasons why they thought the Waverley novels must be by their father, though no one had ever seen a scrap of the manuscript in his handwriting, was that their mother knew all about them, and talked of them, though the copy she was supposed to be reading remained uncut. She seems to be visiting the printing-establishment; at least, it was probably the Ballantyne press they had gone to see on one occasion, when she stained her dress with printer's ink, which nothing would take out.[259]

Charlotte offered her literary assistance whenever she was asked to. As reported by the Scotts' butler at Abbotsford, William Dalgeish, in his 'Memoirs', she was not allowed to enter Scott's study without permission.[260] This is reminiscent of Mr. Oldbuck's sacred '*sanctum sanctorum*', symbolically separated from the rest of the house by a series of thresholds. The antiquarian's study

---

[254] Anderson, 1998: entry 11 May 1826: 163.
[255] Anderson, 1998: entry 16 May 1826: 167.
[256] Anderson, 1998: entry 16 May 1826: 167.
[257] Anderson, 1998: entry 12 June 1826: 180.
[258] Marsch-Caldwell, 1, 1847: 191.
[259] Russell, *Personal History and Associations of Sir Walter Scott*: 41–42.
[260] 'Memoirs of Sir Walter Scott' by William Dalgeish, Scott's butler, 1822–1829', and Mitton, G. E., *Cornhill Magazine*, 70 (Jan.–June 1931), 738 and no. 71 (July–Sept. 1931), 75, 213.

could only be reached 'through a labyrinth of inconvenient and dark passages' and was closed by a door hidden behind 'a piece of tapestry'. In *The Antiquary* (1816), entry is strictly forbidden to 'these cursed womankind' (p. 20), as Oldbuck, Scott's greatest parodic authorial self-portrait, nicknamed his female circle of chambermaid, sister, and niece.

When in charge of proofreading Scott's work, with English not being her mother tongue, Charlotte did not focus on his literary style.[261] Instead, she primarily cross-checked his text for inaccuracies and inconsistencies. In the original manuscript of *The Heart of Midlothian* (Figure 21), fully accessible in digital format on the National Library of Scotland website, there is a small one-page note inserted at the very beginning of the book, before the preliminary address by fictitious Jedidiah Cleishbotham to his readers.[262]

There are clearly two different handwritings on the note. The main one, in ink, is Charlotte's. She points out inconsistencies in character names throughout the story as well as missing paragraphs in the final original manuscript. Her handwriting shows a more flowing, cursive style with noticeable slant and connectivity between letters which are elegant and rounded. Conversely, Scott's handwriting is less slanted, neater, and block-like, with more upright and evenly spaced letters. Writing with a pencil, Scott added a footnote at the bottom of the page ('These are foliations of this MS [manuscript] marked in ink on the inside margins') which he signed 'WS'. Additionally, he corrected Charlotte's note with crosses for annotations and he made changes to her remarks. For example, she had quoted two sentences – written in her usual run-on style without any punctuation mark, which is another grammatical clue identifying her handwriting. The preposition has been crossed out in pencil by Scott and replaced with 'from'. Her first remark is also a bit awkward: 'each time' would have been shorter and more natural in English than 'in each case'.

Charlotte's handwriting is visible in other manuscripts, like in the incomplete manuscript of *Waverley* (Figures 22, 23, 24), with a page written by her, sandwiched between two pages by Scott.[263]

---

[261] 'The secret reason of her procrastination is I believe some terror of writing English, which you know is not her native language,' Scott wrote to Miss Baillie, who had sent Charlotte a thank-you letter for hosting her sister and herself', letter to Joanna Baillie, 18 Sept. 1808, Grierson, 1937–1938: II:90–91.

[262] All the following images Figures 21–25 are reproduced under a Creative Commons Attribution 4.0 International (CC-BY) licence with the permission of the National Library of Scotland. https://creativecommons.org/licenses/by/4.0/. See https://digital.nls.uk/sir-walter-scott/archive.

[263] https://digital.nls.uk/sir-walter-scott/archive.

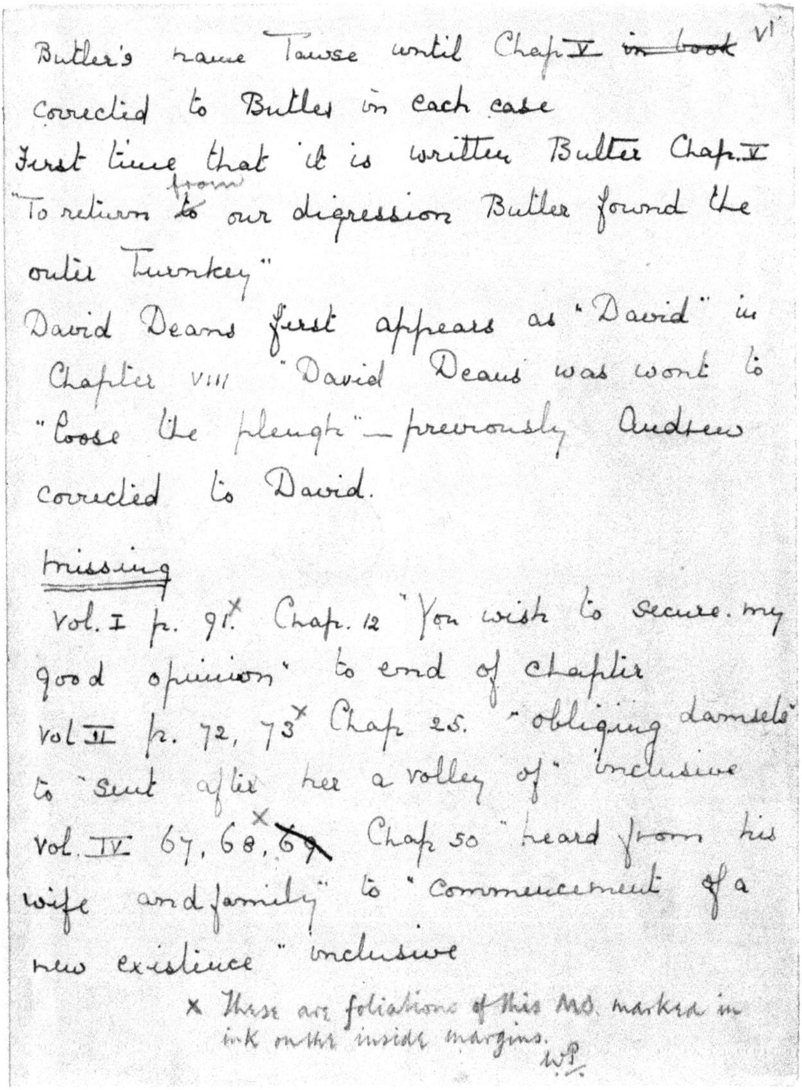

> Butler's name Towse until Chap I in book VI
> Corrected to Butler in each case
> First time that it is written Butler Chap I
> "To return from our digression Butler found the
> outer Turnkey"
> David Deans first appears as "David" in
> Chapter VIII "David Deans was wont to
> "Loose the pleugh" – previously Andrew
> corrected to David.
>
> missing
> Vol. I p. 91ˣ Chap. 12 "You wish to secure my
> good opinion" to end of chapter
> Vol II p. 72, 73ˣ Chap. 25. "obliging damsels"
> to "sent after her a volley of" inclusive
> Vol. IV 67, 68, 69ˣ Chap 50 "heard from his
> wife and family" to "Commencement of a
> new existence" inclusive
>   ˣ These are foliations of this MS. marked in
>   ink on the inside margins. WS.

Figure 21 *The Heart of Midlothian*, original manuscript: 13.

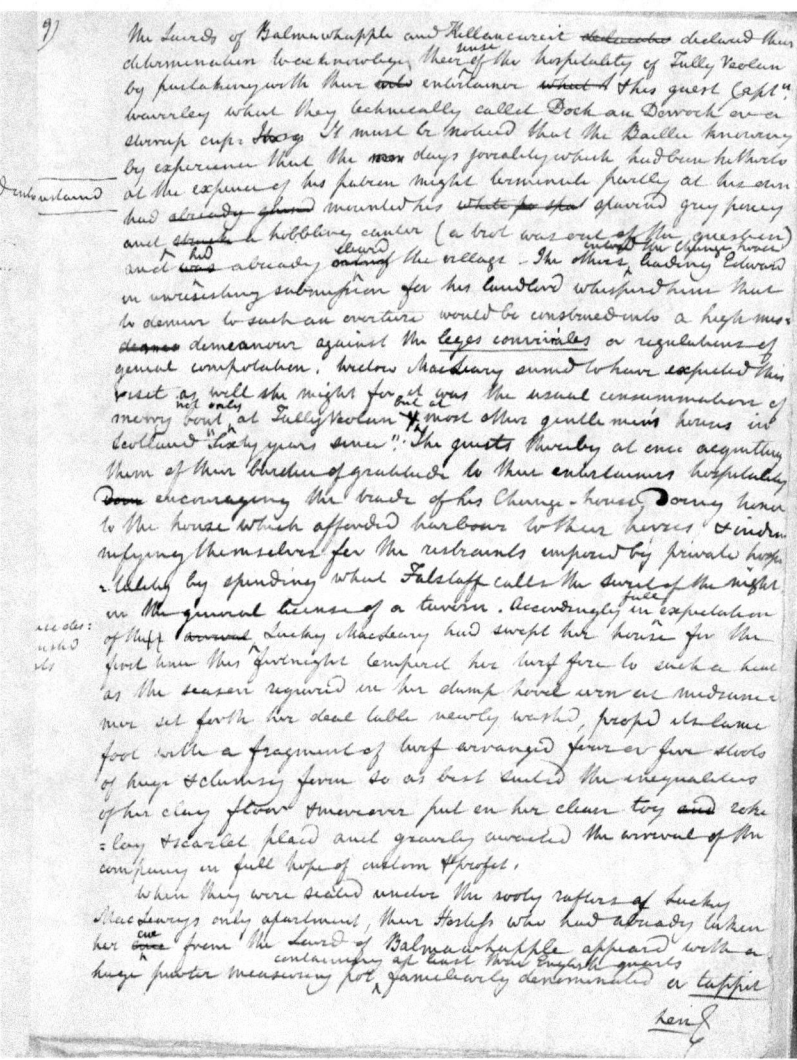

Figure 22 *Waverley*, Scott, [1814] (2007): 105.

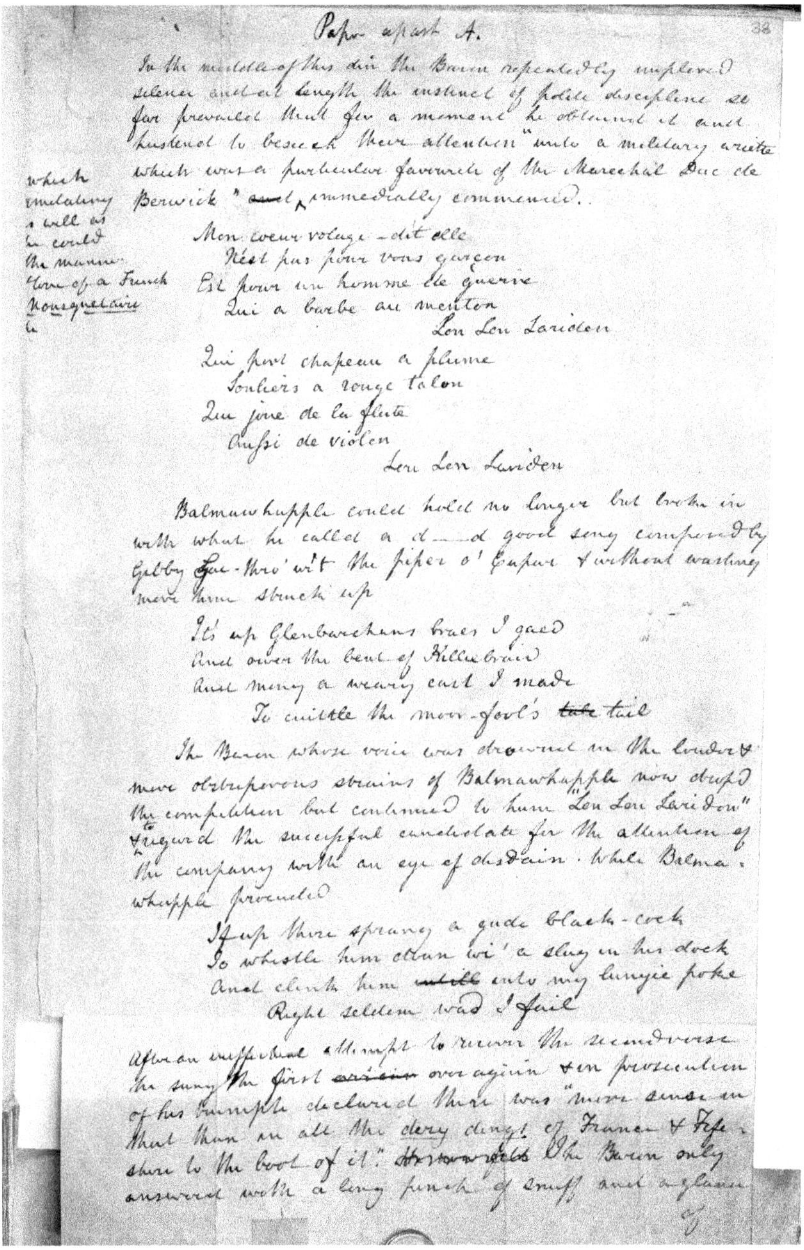

Figure 23 *Waverley*, Scott, [1814] (2007): 107.

and which in the language of the house ream'd (i.e. mantled) with excellent claret just drawn from the cask. It was soon plain that what crumbs of reason the Bear had not devoured were to be picked up by the Hen; but the confusion which began to prevail favoured Edwards resolution to evade the gaily circling glass. The rest began to talk thick and at once each performing his own tune without the least respect to his neighbour. The Baron of Bradwardine sung french chansons a boire & spouted pieces of Latin, Killancureit talked in a steady unaltera=ble dull key of top-dressing and bottom-dressing & year-olds and gimmers & dinmonts and stots and runts & kyloes & a proposed turnpike act while Balmawhapple in notes exalted above both extolled his horse his hawks and a greyhound called Whistler. But alas! the Demon of politics envied even the harmony arising from this Dutch concert merely because there was not a wrathful note in the strange compound of sounds which it produced. Inspired by her the Laird of Balmawhapple now superior to the nods and winks with which the Baron of Bradwardine in delicacy to Edward had hitherto checked his entering upon political discussion de=manded a bumper with the lungs of a Stentor "to the little gentleman in black velvet who did such service in 1702 and may the White Horse break his neck over a mound of his making." Edward was not at that moment clear-headed enough to remember that King Williams fall which occasioned his death was said to be owing to his horse stum=bling at a mole-hill yet he felt inclined to take umbrage at a toast which seemed from the glance of Balmawhapples eye to bear a peculiar & uncivil reference to the government. But ere he could interfere the Baron of Bradwardine had taken up the quarrel. "Sir whatever my sentiments tanquam privatus may be in such matters I shall not tamely endure your saying any thing that may impinge upon the honourable feelings of a gentleman under my roof. Sir if you have no respect for the laws of urbanity do ye not respect the milita=ry oath the sacramentum militare by which every officer

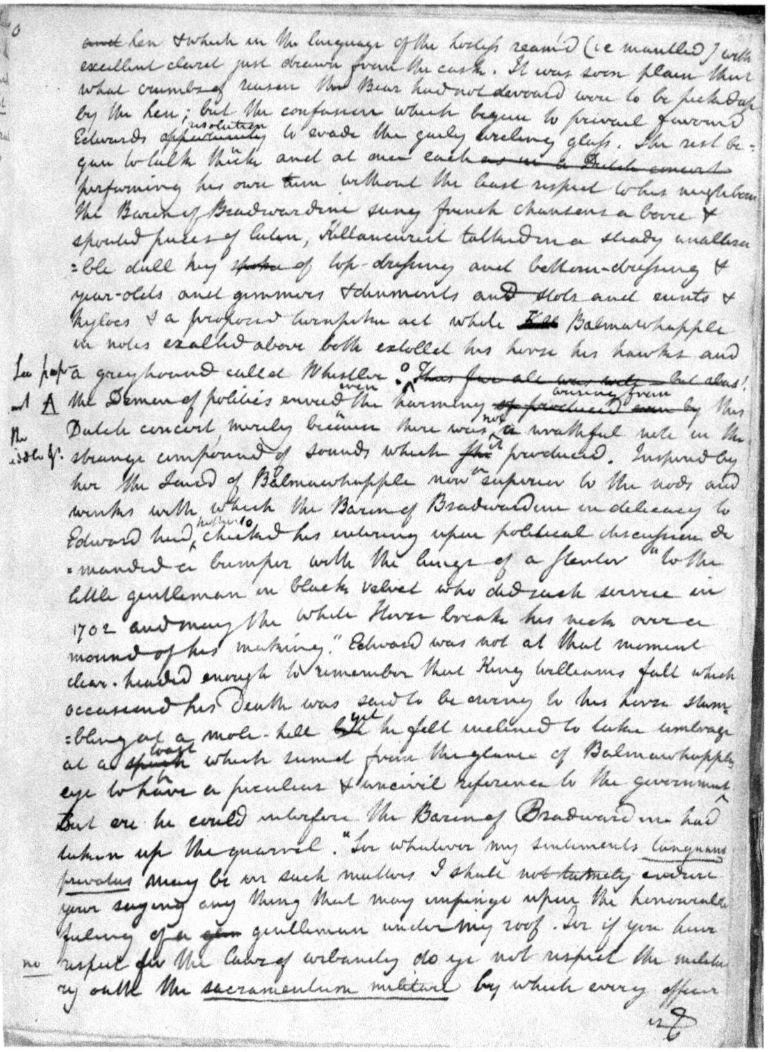

Figure 24 *Waverley*, Scott, [1814] (2007): 109.

"Fergus Mac Ivor of Glennaquoich otherwise called Vich Ian Vohr and Evan MacIvor in the Dhu of Tarrascleugh otherwise called Evan Dhu, otherwise called Evan Maccombich or Evan Dhu Maccombich You and each of you stand attainted of High Treason. What have you to say for yourselves why the Court should not pronounce judgement against you, that you die according to law?"

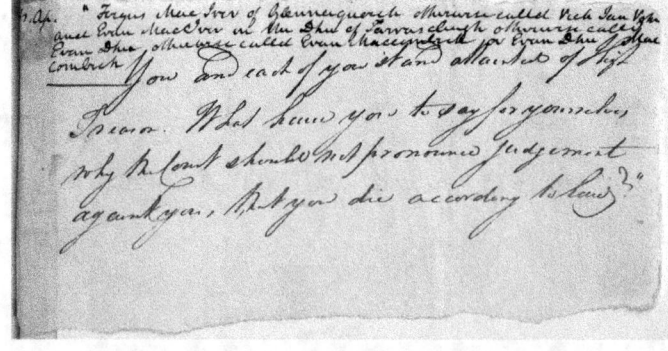

Figure 25 *Waverley*, Scott, [1814] (2007): 455.

Similarly, a note on page 455 (Figure 25) contains two different handwritings. The first has a more uniform and consistent flow,[264] while the second is more spaced out.[265]

On top of Charlotte, other women in his literary circle of proofreaders were responsible for commenting on the plot structure and the overall cohesion, pacing, characterisation, dialogue, theme, setting, and narrative voice. Elizabeth Leveson-Gower, Duchess of Sutherland and patron of the arts,[266] Lady Louisa Stuart,[267] and Scottish poet and dramatist Joanna Baillie – the only literary woman in his circle of proofreaders from 1815 – were among the few, with Charlotte, who knew Scott was the Author of *Waverley*. Drafts of *The Lord of the Isles* (1815) are discussed in his correspondence with Baillie from 1808 to 1810, while in 1808 she also thanked Scott for 'the confidence you have put in me [and] the high gratifications I have had in reading The House of Aspen', eventually published in 1829.[268] She stressed the similarities with parts of her tragedy, playfully dodging any imaginary charges of plagiarism:

> Do you know! I have a tragedy at home in which a wife discovers the guilt of her husband, by the dying confession of a servant who was present at the crime, and I have scenes afterwards between her & the husband in which she tries to discover whether he is really guilty or not. Don't after this think, if you should see it, that I have borrowed the idea from you; it has been long written and is now in the hands of Mr Baillie; and if you should ever work up this part of your piece more fully, it may be an amusement to us some time or other to compare the two plays in this respect together. I will not let you beat me on my own ground if I can help it; but, if it must be so, I will less grudgingly yield the victory to you than any other Poet I know of.[269]

Scott thus greatly benefitted from these literary exchanges on his in-progress manuscripts with this circle of women whose candid criticisms he highly valued and whose works he read and critiqued in return. As part of his support network and literary coterie, these female proofreaders also took any negative criticism of his work to heart, feeling personally targeted by the critics. Hence Charlotte's

---

[264] 'Fergus Mac-Ivor of Glennaquoich, otherwise called Vich Ian Vohr, and Evan Mac-Ivor, in the Dhu of Tarrascleugh, otherwise called Evan Dhu, otherwise called Evan Maccombich, or Evan Dhu MacCombich', Scott, 1814: 341.

[265] This is the rest of the sentence '–you, and each of you, stand attainted of high treason. What have you to say for yourselves why the Court should not pronounce judgment against you, that you die according to law?', Scott, 1814: 341.

[266] 'My dear Lady Stafford, – I am much honoured by your attaching any value to the Lord of the Isles, which I think will be the last poem I shall attempt upon any scale of length or subject of importance,' letter to Elizabeth, Marchioness of Stafford, 21 Jan. 1815, Grierson, 1937–1938: IV:20.

[267] See his letter to Lady Louisa Stuart on *Marmion*, 19 Jan. 1808, Grierson, 1937–1938: II.3.

[268] Letter from Joanna Baillie to Walter Scott, 31 Oct. 1808, Grierson, 1937–1938: II:116; Letter from Joanna Baillie to Walter Scott, 10 June 1810, Grierson, 1937–1938: II:349.

[269] 'Letters chiefly of Sir Walter Scott, 1792–1817'.

resentment towards Francis Jeffrey, the editor of the prestigious *Edinburgh Review*, 'arch-critic'[270] and friend of Scott, after he wrote a very negative review of *Marmion* in his journal.[271]

'Unveiling Lady Scott', to borrow the title of this Element, means revealing her as Scott's indispensable partner in every aspect of life and work, serving as his stage and literary manager – in charge of the family's hospitality and keeping the secret of his authorship – and as his muse, scribe, research assistant, and proofreader. In essence, 'unveiling Lady Scott' is recognising that she supported and encouraged him, providing the assistance and guidance that humbly fuelled his prolific and innovative literary output. As his steadfast supporter from the very beginning, she was the one who encouraged his writing ambitions, as attested by her prophetic letter[272] to her guardian, Arthur Hill, in May 1800: 'Scott is not idle, for he is trying to make up for it by employing his Pen which I think will prove more profitable than the Law at present.'[273] She could not have been more right.

Conclusion

'Who was Lady Scott originally?' This question, posed by James Hogg, initiated my exploration, though I soon realised that it was not the right question to ask. Instead of focusing solely on descent, birth, and lineage (the etymological meanings of 'origin'), I believe it is more insightful to consider how she grew into her transnational and transcultural identity. The term 'origin' is better understood in its figurative meaning: 'to arise, to lift, to raise, to set in motion, to move'. Lady Scott's story is a matter of contruction, both in the sense of personal and social growth, and as a literary composition. To the eyes of Scott's critics and biographers, she has been transformed into a fictional character, a fairy tale heroine. In their stereotypical narratives, she has become the orphan of a wayward mother (Mrs Volere, that is *Volage* to play on words) and a ruined father, taken in by a benevolent and philanthropic Irish count. These writers have admittedly crafted 'Romances' or proposed compelling intricate narratives, filling in the gaps with figments of their imagination, 'speculating' (in their own words) to complete the blanks in her story.[274] Ironically, in accusing

---

[270] It is a nickname Scott gave to literary critic George Ellis. Grierson, Letter to Ellis, 19 May 1804, Grierson, 1937–1938: I:222.

[271] 'Mrs Scott, although perfectly polite, was not quite as easy with him as usual. When her guests were leaving, "Well, good night, Mr Jeffrey – dey tell me you have abused Scott in de Review, and I hope Mr Constable has paid you very well for writing it,"' Dexter, 1960: 54.

[272] This was one of her prophetic letters since, writing to Scott on 29 Nov. 1797, she had also said 'I have no doubt but that you will rise very high, and be a <u>great rich man</u>,' 'Letters chiefly of Sir Walter Scott, 1792–1817'.

[273] 'Letters chiefly of Sir Walter Scott, 1792–1817'.

[274] Bigger, *Belfast News-Letter*, Saturday, 14 Oct. 1922.

one another of offering a sanitised, romanticised version of reality, they have been ensnared by fiction themselves. In trying to water down or dramatise her story, they have unwittingly misled themselves and fallen into the trap of romance. Charlotte Charpentier was not the plain, uneducated provincial Frenchwoman of obscure origins with a heavy accent, akin to an ancestral figure of Cosette in Hugo's *Les Misérables*.

To prove this, I studied previously unearthed archival materials from France and Scotland, particularly from the National Library of Scotland, the Edinburgh University Library, and the Abbotsford Collection stored at both Abbotsford Library and the Signet Library in Edinburgh. I also cross-examined letters, journals, and diaries from French and international literary guests at Abbotsford, demonstrating her active engagement in literary discussions. Besides, through detailed literary micro-readings of Scott's fictions, complemented by an extensive reading of his autobiographical writings, such as his letters and journal, I have revealed for the first time in this Element that Lady Scott not only inspired several of Scott's female characters, such as Julia Mannering and Rose Bradwardine, but also embodied a cross-gender archetype for his male heroes like Edward Waverley, Frank Osbaldistone, and Guy Mannering.

In crafting this counter-narrative that revisits the sources and explores new ones with a unique comparative approach, my aim was to unveil Lady Scott's dual origins, underscoring her profoundly transnational and transcultural position. She had biological roots in Lyon, France, at a once internationally renowned royal centre of excellence that was in decline on the eve of the French Revolution. Additionally, she had an adoptive background in London, where she lived with a prominent French-born family and under the protection of an influential Irish lord who was nevertheless burdened with debts and eventually stripped of all honours for opposing the union of Great Britain and Ireland in 1800. Consistently navigating a state of in-betweenness among cultures French and English, then French and Scottish – across social statuses of rich and poor, and between countries, she eventually settled at Abbotsford, in a region straddling the border between England and Scotland.

Her meeting and marriage to Walter Scott, who was to become a global literary figure, was no coincidence. Instead, it was the inevitable culmination of her distinctive life story and personal development. It was a gradual journey that prepared her for social ascension and northward relocation, as well as a life dedicated in her husband's shadow, where she played significant roles as his creative supporter and literary assistant.[275] This gradual development reflects a continuous learning and apprenticeship that followed her journey from France

---

[275] Duncan, 2007.

Figure 26 Charlotte and Walter Scott's tombstone at Dryburgh Abbey. Credit to Historic Environment Scotland.

to England, and finally to Scotland, mirroring the paths taken by many of Walter Scott's protagonists in his novels.

Though previously uncommented upon, it is noteworthy that in 1846, a monumental tombstone for both Walter Scott and his wife was erected (Figure 26).[276] It features two adjoining compartments, with one bearing the inscription 'Dame Charlotte Margaret Carpenter, wife of Sir Walter Scott of Abbotsford'.

Commissioned by the Lockharts with Robert Cadell's assistance, this engraving is significant because it is the first and only time the title 'Dame' was used for Scott's wife, who was officially known as 'Lady'. This choice, etched in stone for eternity, strongly implies a posthumous recognition of her personal achievements. The engraving further combines her French and English first names and anglicises her maiden name, thus highlighting her transcultural identity.

Scott famously drew inspiration from female authors, with his style reflecting the sentimental tradition and gothic romance, as seen in *The Mysteries of Udolpho* (1794), of Ann Radcliffe, whom he admired as 'the mighty enchantress', and the regional novels of Maria Edgeworth. Moreover, his fiction was significantly inspired by his Scottish female contemporaries, such as Joanna Baillie, Mary Brunton, Susan Ferrier, and Jane Porter.[277] Porter's *Thaddeus of*

---

[276] The *Glasgow Herald* broke the news on 16 Oct. 1846 and this article was followed by eight others in Scottish newspapers.
[277] Monnickendam, 2013.

Warsaw (1803) and *The Highland Chiefs: A Romance* (1810) were among the early historical novels that profoundly influenced Scott's *Waverley* (1814). I have ultimately demonstrated that Lady Scott was an essential bridge between different circles, largely composed of women. On one side was the Scott family – with their daughters, Sophia and Anne, who also served as hostesses and scribes, and in Sophia's case, as guardian of their father's literary heritage, following in the footsteps of the family's female storytellers. On the other side was Scott's literary coterie, a supportive network of publishers, printers, antiquarians, collectors, and writers – again, partly female – as discussed throughout this Element.

This essential narrative, published just before the bicentenary of Lady Scott's death in 2026, provides an opportunity to re-examine Scott's works through the lens of his French and transnational connections. It challenges the conventional view of Scott as a Scottish icon focused on nationalistic (more cultural than political) themes and Scotland's distinctiveness within the United Kingdom. While his dedication to Scotland's history and heritage is undeniable, this Element underscores his significant European ties and transnational connections, particularly through his wife, suggesting that he was far less exclusively Scottish or even British than sometimes perceived. This approach – building on the work of Murray Pittock in *Reception of Sir Walter Scott in Europe* – is particularly compelling given the current interest in global and cross-cultural studies. I sincerely hope this study encourages further research into Scott's transcultural approach to history in his fiction, as well as the indirect influence of his close social circle and literary coterie in shaping which British writers were translated into French and made accessible to readers in France. This affected the international circulation and reach of these works.

This Element also aims to make a meaningful contribution to the growing field of Franco-British study and work on women writers from the Revolutionary era to the 1830s. Building on the research of European history specialists such as Kirsty Carpenter, Juliette Reboul, Philip Mansel, Simon Burrows, and Friedemann Pestel, this Element explores the connections between France and Britain's literary traditions through the case study of Lady Scott, within the framework of the 'Eighteenth-Century Connections' series. It is part of a broader, ongoing study of the transnational circulation of literature and culture between the two countries, and the role played by often polyglot agents of exchange – assistants, proofreaders, printers, editors, translators, or *salonnières*. Despite a vibrant traffic in the written word and in cultural forms that often defied and transcended national boundaries, national canons have largely remained distinct – at least until recently – and much work remains to be done to unsettle or dismantle them.

Bibliography

Primary Sources

Anderson, William E. K. *The Journal of Sir Walter Scott*. London: Canongate Classics, 1998.

Charpentié, Jean François. *Académie du roi, de Lyon*. Lyon: Aimé de la Roche, 1771.

Hyde, Mary Morley Crapo. *The Thrales of Streatham Park*. Cambridge, MA: Harvard University Press, 1977. https://archive.org/details/thralesofstreath00hest/mode/2up.

Irving, Pierre M. *The Life and Letters of Washington Irving*. New York: G. P. Putnam, 1862.

Nodier, Charles. *Promenade de Dieppe aux montagnes d'Écosse*. Paris: J.-N. Barba, 1821. https://gallica.bnf.fr/ark:/12148/bpt6k617905/f162.item.

Sainte-Beuve, *Oeuvres*. Paris: Gallimard, 1949–1951.

Scott, Walter. [1814] (2007). *Waverley*. Edinburgh: Edinburgh University Press.

[1805] *The Lay of the last Minstrel*. Canto fifth, XIII. London: Longman.

[1815] (1999). *Guy Mannering*. Edinburgh: Edinburgh University Press.

[1816] (1995). *The Antiquary*. Edinburgh: Edinburgh University Press.

(1816). *Guy Mannering*. Translated by Joseph Martin. Paris: Plancher.

[1817] (2008). *Rob Roy*. Edinburgh: Edinburgh University Press.

(1817). *L'Antiquaire*. Translated by Sophie de Maraise. Paris: Antoine Béraud.

[1818] (2004). *The Heart of Mid-Lothian*. Edinburgh: Edinburgh University Press.

[1819] (1996). *The Bride of Lammermoor*. Edinburgh: Edinburgh University Press.

[1824] (1997). *Redgauntlet*. Edinburgh: Edinburgh University Press.

Letters

Corson, James C. *Notes and Index to Sir Herbert Grierson's Edition of the Letters of Sir Walter Scott*. Oxford: Clarendon Press, 1979.

Douglas, David. *Familiar Letters of Sir Walter Scott*, by Walter Scott. Edinburgh: David Douglas, 1894.

Grierson, Herbert Sir. *The Letters of Sir Walter Scott*. 12 vols. London: Constable, 1932–1937. www.walterscott.lib.ed.ac.uk/etexts/etexts/letters.html.

Letters, Hithertho Unpublished, Written by Members of Sir Walter Scott's Family to Their Old Governess. London: Grant Richards, 1905.

Millgate Union Catalogue of Walter Scott Correspondence. https://digital.nls.uk/catalogues/walter-scott-correspondence/bio/?id=34.

Montagu, Lady Mary Wortley. *The Letters of Lady M. W. Montagu during the Embassy to Constantinople, 1716–1718*. Vol. 1. London: John Sharpe, 1820.

Partington, Wilfred. *The Private Letter-Books of Sir Walter Scott (1799–1831): Selections from the Abbotsford Manuscripts, with a Letter to the Reader from Hugh Walpole*. London: Hodder and Stoughton, 1930.

Sir Walter's Post-Bag: More Stories and Sidelights from His Unpublished Letter-Books. London: John Murray, 1932.

Petty-Fitzmaurice, Henry E. *The Queeney Letters: Being Letters Addressed to Hester Maria Thrale*. London: Cassell & Company, 1934. https://archive.org/details/queeneyletters0000unse/page/n5/mode/2up.

Scott, Walter. *The Letters of Sir Walter Scott: E-text*. www.walterscott.lib.ed.ac.uk/etexts/etexts/letters.html.

Archives

Almanach astronomique et historique de la ville de Lyon, et des provinces de Lyonnois, Forez et Beaujolois; Pour l'Année Bissextile 1788. Vol. 71. Lyon: J. H. Duval, 1788. https://bit.ly/3IWIV9l.

Almanach civil, politique et littéraire de Lyon et du département du Rhône. 1743. https://bit.ly/4ogwK7B.

Almanach de la ville de Lyon. Lyon: Aimé de la Roche, 1772.

The East India Kalendar; or, Asiatic Register for Bengal, Madras, Bombay, Fort Marlborough, China, and St. Helena. For the Year 1797. Edinburgh: National Library of Scotland, 1797.

The Eton College Register, 1753–1790: Alphabetically Arranged and Edited with Biographical Notes, ed. Richard Arthur Austen-Leigh, 1921. https://bit.ly/3GUZ2DU.

'Dumergue's Divorce Bill', *Journals of the House of Lords*, no. 35 (1779).

Fox, Henry Edward. *The Journal of Henry Edward Fox (afterwards fourth and last Lord Holland), 1818–1830*. Ed. the Earl of Ilchester. London: Thornton Butterworth Limited, 1923. www.archive.org/details/journalofhenryed00holluoft.

House of Lords Journal 35 (June 1779): 1–10. www.british-history.ac.uk/lords-jrnl/vol35/pp767-788.

'Letters of Denisation and Acts of Naturalisation for Aliens in England and Ireland, 1701–1800'. *The Publications of the Huguenot Society of London*. Manchester: Sherrat and Hughes, 1923.

Parliamentary Archives: 'Dissolution of Marriage Petition', HL_PO_JO_10_272_4; 'Marriage Dissolution Bill', HL_PO_JO_10_7_596.

Procès-verbaux des séances des Corps municipaux de la ville de Lyon, publiés par la Municipalité, d'après les manuscrits originaux, 1787-an VIII, vol. 1. Lyon, 1899.

Record of Services of the Honourable East India Company's Civil Servants in the Madras Presidency, from 1741 to 1858, ed. Charles Campbell Prinsep. London: Trübner, 1885. https://archive.org/details/recordofservices00prinrich.

Abbotsford Collection

'Abbotsford Plans', T.A.D.1354.1.

Bürger, Gottfried August. *Leonora*, 1796. Z.2.5.

The Eve of St John: A Border Ballad. Signet Library, Edinburgh.

Surenne, Gabriel. *Practical Grammar or French Rhetoric*. Edinburgh, 1824. L.3:13.

National Library of Scotland

'Correspondence, 1930–1935, of James Glen, Writer, Glasgow, chiefly with Professor Sir Herbert Grierson', MS.2566.

'Letter of Sir Walter Scott to Mrs Hamilton Sending of Copy of the "Lay of the Last Minstrel"' for Miss Carmichael, MS.23141, ff. 30–31.

'Letter of Sir Walter Scott to Lady Douglas, Sending Proofs of "The Lay of the Last Minstrel"', MS.2311, f. 90.

'Letters chiefly of Sir Walter Scott, 1792–1817', James Glen Memorial Collection, MS. 2525.

'Letters of Sir Walter Scott to His Wife on His Travel Plans', Acc. 14307.

Material relating to Sir Walter Scott and Robert Southey, Written and Collected by James Glen, Writer, Glasgow. MS.S.2525–2533.

'"Memoirs of Sir Walter Scott" by William Dalgeish, Scott's Butler, 1822–1829', MS.5199.

Russell, Helen J. M. *The Personal History and Associations of Sir Walter Scott*, mid-nineteenth century, MS. 3234.

British Newspaper Articles; British National Archives

Atlas: A General Newspaper and Journal of Literature. London, Sun. 11 Nov. 1832.

Bigger, Francis Joseph. 'Sir Walter Scott's Romance'. *Belfast News-Letter* (Sat. 14 Oct. 1922).

Bolton Free Press (Sat. 25 March 1837).

Buchan, John. *The Week-End Review*, quoted in *The Scotsman* (Thurs. 17 July 1930): 2.
Carswell, Donald. 'Who Was Lady Scott?' *The Statesman* (Thurs. 17 July 1930).
'Lady Scott's Origins'. *The Scotsman* (Sat. 22 Nov. 1930).
Crockett, Dr. William Shillinglaw. 'Sir Walter: Who Was Lady Scott?' *The Scotsman* (Sat. 12 July 1930a).
'Lady Scott's Origins', *The Scotsman* (Fri. 5 Dec. 1930b).
'New Light on Lady Scott: Fresh Documents'. *The Scotsman* (Sat. 18 April 1931): 12.
Grierson, Herbert Sir. 'Lady Scott's Family: Who was Margaret Charpentier?' *The Scotsman* (Sat. 15 Nov. 1930).
John Bull (Sunday newspaper). London: Edward Shackell, 1820–1892.
Johnston, James B. 'Lady Scott'. *The Scotsman* (Thurs. 17 July 1930).
'The Late Lady Scott'. *Manchester Courier* (Sat. 17 Nov. 1832).
Liverpool Albion (Mon. 27 March 1837).
Mitton, Geraldine E. *Cornhill Magazine*, no. 70 (Jan.–June 1931): 738 and no. 71 (July–Sept. 1931): 75, 213.
Oman, Carola. 'The True Scott'. *Illustrated London News* (1 Aug. 1971).
'Sir Walter Scott's Connection with Cumberland'. *Carlisle Patriot* (Fri. 28 July 1871): 4.
'Sir Walter Scott's Courtship'. *Bolton Free Press* (Sat. 25 March 1837): 4.
'Sir Walter Scott's First and Second Love'. *Liverpool Albion* (Mon. 27 March 1837): 7.
'Walter Scott and Scottish History and Character'. *Comoedia* (Fri. 22 April 1932).

French Newspaper Articles; Retronews

Descoux, Philippe. 'Walter Scott'. *Les Contemporains*, no.118 (13 jan. 1895).
'Feuilleton: Conseils de Walter Scott à son fils'. *Journal de Paris* (dim. 3 sept. 1837): 1–3.
'Feuilleton: Correspondance littéraire de Walter Scott'. *Journal de Paris*, (3 déc. 1837): 1–3.
Le Figaro (28 sept. 1832).
Gazette de France, no. 283 (11 oct. 1809).
Gazette nationale ou le Moniteur universel, no. 56 (25 fév. 1810): 1.
Gazette nationale ou le Moniteur universel, no. 243 (31 août 1811): 4.
Gazette nationale ou le Moniteur universel, 1813.
Journal des arts et de la politique, 1815.
Journal des débats politiques et littéraires (30 mars 1877): 3.

Journal de l'Empire (27 juil. 1812): 3.
Journal de l'Empire, 1813.
Journal Général de France, 1816.
Journal de Paris, 1813.
Journal de Paris (dim. 3 déc. 1837): 293.
'Lady Scott'. *Excelsior* (1 oct. 1932).
Martin-Basse. 'La femme de Walter Scott'. *Journal des débats politiques et littéraires* (21 sept. 1932).
'Mémoires sur la vie de Walter Scott, par J. G. Lockhart'. Supplément au Journal *Le Constitutionnel*, no. 294 (21 oct. 1838): 7–8.
Mercure de France, 1813.
La Quotidienne, 1816.
Roth, Georges. 'Walter Scott et la France ... de son temps'. *La Grande Revue* (1 déc. 1932): 189–212.
'Walter Scott: son enfance et sa jeunesse racontée par lui-même'. Supplément au Journal *Le Constitutionnel*, no. 287 (30 av. 1837): 5–6.

Secondary Sources

Biographies of Scott

Alexander, John H. and David Hewitt. *Scott and His Influence*. Aberdeen: Association for Scottish Literary Studies, 1983.
Allan, George. *Life of Sir Walter Scott, Baronet: With Critical Notices of His Writings*. Edinburgh: Thomas Ireland Junior, 1834.
Bell, Alan. *Scott Bicentenary Essays*. Edinburgh: Scottish Academic Press, 1973.
Bold, Alan. *Sir Walter Scott: The Long-Forgotten Melody*. London: Barnes and Noble, 1983.
Buchan, John. *Sir Walter Scott*. London: Cassell, 1932. https://bit.ly/3UFoal7.
Carswell, Donald. *Sir Walter: A Four-Part Study in Biography (Scott, Hogg, Lockhart, Baillie)*. London: John Murray, 1930. https://archive.org/details/sirwalterfourpar0000dona/page/n5/mode/2up.
Chambers, Robert. *Life of Sir Walter Scott*. Edinburgh: W. and R. Chambers, 1871. www.gutenberg.org/cache/epub/69330/pg69330-images.html.
Clark, Arthur Melville. *Walter Scott: The Formative Years*. Edinburgh: Blackwood, 1969.
Cunningham, Allan. *Some Account of the Life and Works of Sir Walter Scott*. Boston, MA: Stimpson and Clapp, 1832.
Daiches, David. *Sir Walter Scott and His World*. London: Thames and Hudson, 1971.

Dunlop, Eileen. *Sir Walter Scott: A Life in Story*. Edinburgh: National Museums of Scotland, 2016.

Findlay, Jessie Patrick. *Sir Walter Scott: The Great Unknown*. Edinburgh: Nimmo, Hay and Mitchell, 1912.

Fowler, Wright Sydney. *The Life of Sir Walter Scott*. New York: Haskell House, 1932.

Gillies, Robert Pearse. *Recollections of Sir Walter Scott*. London: James Fraser, 1837.

Grierson, Elizabeth W. *Sir Walter Scott*. London: Black, 1913.

Grierson, Herbert, Sir. *Sir Walter Scott, Bart.: A New Life supplementary to, and corrective of, Lockhart's Biography*. London: Constable, 1938.

Gwynn, Stephen. *The Life of Sir Walter Scott*. London: Thornton, 1930.

Hewitt, David. *Scott on Himself: A Selection of the Autobiograhical Writings of Sir Walter Scott*. Edinburgh: Scottish Academic Press, 1981.

Hogg, James. *Familiar Anecdotes of Sir Walter Scott*. New York: Harper and Brothers, 1834.

Hudson, William Henry. *Sir Walter Scott*. London: Sands, 1901. https://archive.org/stream/sirwalterscott01hudsgoog/sirwalterscott01hudsgoog_djvu.txt.

Hutchinson, Horace G. *Letters and Recollections of Sir Walter Scott by Mrs Hughes (of Uffington)*. London: Smith, Elder and Company, 1904.

Hutton, Richard Holt. *Sir Walter Scott*. London: Macmillan, 1878.

Jeffares, A. Norman. *Scott's Mind and Art*. Edinburgh: Oliver and Boyd, 1969.

Johnson, Edgar. *Sir Walter Scott: The Great Unknown*. London: H. Hamilton, 1970.

Lang, Andrew. *Sir Walter Scott*. London: Hodder and Stoughton, 1906.

Lauber, John. *Sir Walter Scott*. Boston, MA: Twayne, 1989.

Lockhart, John Gibson. *Memoirs of the Life of Sir Walter Scott*. Vol. 1. Edinburgh: Cadell, 1837–1838. https://lordbyron.org/monograph.php?doc=JoLockh.Scott&select=I.ch8.

MacMaster, Graham. *Scott and Society*. Cambridge: Cambridge University Press, 1981.

MacNalty, Arthur Salusbury. *Sir Walter Scott: The Wounded Falcon*. London: Johnson, 1969.

Matthew, George King. *Abbotsford and Sir Walter Scott*. Edinburgh: Oliver and Boyd, 1854.

Millgate, Jane. *Walter Scott: The Making of the Novelist*. Edinburgh: Edinburgh University Press, 1984.

Norgate, Gerald le Grys. *The Life of Sir Walter Scott*. London: Methuen and Company, 1906. https://archive.org/details/thelifeofsirwalt00norguoft.

Oman, Carola. *The Wizard of the North: The Life of Sir Walter Scott*. London: Hodder and Stoughton, 1973.

Palgrave, Francis Turner. *Life of Sir Walter: With Remarks upon His Writings*. Philadelphia, PA: Porter and Coates, 1871. https://digital.nls.uk/antiquarian-books-of-scotland/archive/114200414#?cv=31.

Partington, Wilfred. *Sir Walter's Post-Bag: More Stories and Sidelights from Unpublished Letter-books*. London: John Murray, 1932.

Pearson, Hersketh. *Walter Scott: His Life and Personality*. London: Methuen, 1954.

Pope-Hennessy, Una, Dame. *The Laird of Abbotsford: An Informal Presentation of Sir Walter Scott*. London: Putnam, 1932.

Sir Walter Scott. London: Home and Van Thal, 1948.

Quayle, Eric. *The Ruin of Sir Walter Scott*. London: Rupert Hart-Davis, 1968.

Robertson, Fiona. *Lives of the Great Romantics II: Scott* . Vol. 3. London: Routledge, 1997.

Rogers, Charles. *Genealogical Memoirs of the Family of Sir Walter Scott, Bart. of Abbortsford, with a Reprint of the Memorials of the Haliburtons*. London: Houston and Sons, 1877. https://digital.nls.uk/dcn6/7940/79403684.6.pdf.

Saintsbury, George. *Sir Walter Scott*. Edinburgh: Oliphant Anderson and Ferrier, 1897.

Salusbury, Arthur, Sir. *Sir Walter Scott: The Wounded Falcon*. London: Johnson, 1969.

Schultz, Pearle H. *Sir Walter Scott: The Wizard of the North*. New York: Vanguard Press, 1967.

Scott, Adam. *The Story of Sir Walter Scott's First Love*. Edinburgh: Macniven and Wallace, 1896.

Skene, James. *Memories of Sir Walter Scott*. London: J. Murray, 1909. https://archive.org/details/memoriesofsirwal00skenuoft.

Suhamy, Henri. *Sir Walter Scott*. Paris: Édition de Fallois, 1993.

Walter Scott: Inventeur du roman historique. Paris: La Nouvelle Librairie, 2022.

Sultana, Donald. *From Abbotsford to Paris and Back: Sir Walter Scott's Journey of 1815*. Gloucestershire: Alan Sutton, 1993.

Sutherland, John. *The Life of Walter Scott: A Critical Biography*. Oxford: Blackwell, 1995.

Wright, Sydney Fowler. *The Life of Sir Walter Scott*. New York: Haskell House, 1932.

Books

Adam, Thomas. *Yearbook of Transnational History*. Vol. 4. London: Fairleigh Dickinson University Press, 2021.

Agier, Michel and Anne-Virginie Madeira. *Définir les réfugiés*. Paris: Presses Universitaires de France, 2017.

Andress, David. *The Routledge Handbook of French History*. Abingdon: Routledge, 2024.

Armitage, David and Sanjay Subrahmanyam. *The Age of Revolutions in Global Context, c. 1760–1840*. Basingstoke: Palgrave Macmillan, 2010.

Balderston, Katharine Canby. *Thraliana, the Diary of Mrs Hester Lynch Thrale, later Mrs Piozzi*, 1776–1809. Vol. 1. Oxford: Clarendon Press, 1942.

Baudino, Isabelle. *Les Voyageuses britanniques au 18e siècle: l'étape lyonnaise dans l'itinéraire du Grand Tour*. Paris: L'Harmattan, 2015. https://doi/org/10.4000/1718.323.

Beauvoir, Simone de. *Le deuxième sexe*. 2 tomes. Paris: Gallimard, 1949.

Bernard, Claudie. *Le Passé recomposé: Le roman historique français du dix-neuvième siècle*. Paris: Hachette, 1996.

Bertrand, Gilles. *Le Grand Tour revisité: Le voyage des Français en Italie*. Rome: École française de Rome, 2021.

Boucher-Rivalain, Odile et Catherine Hajdenko-Marshall. *Regards des Anglo-Saxons sur la France au cours du long 19e siècle*. Paris: L'Harmattan, 2008.

Broadie, Alexandre. *Agreeable Connexions: Scottish Enlightenment Links with France*. Edinburgh: John Donald, 2012.

Butler, Marilyn. *Maria Edgeworth: A Literary Biography*. Oxford: Clarendon Press, 1972.

Carpenter, Kirsty. *Refugees of the French Revolution: Émigrés in London, 1789–1802*. Houndmills: Palgrave Macmillan, 1999.

Carpenter, Kirsty and Philip Mansel. *The French Émigrés in Europe and the Struggle against Revolution, 1789–1814*. Houndmills: Palgrave Macmillan, 1999.

Cornick, Martyn. 'Introduction. The French in London: A Study in Time and Space'. In Debra Kelly and Martyn Cornick, eds. *A History of the French in London*. London: University of London Press, 2013, 1–12. www.jstor.org/stable/j.ctv512xmz.

Crockett, William Shillinglaw. *The Scott Country*. Edinburgh: Adam and Charles Black, 1911.

Beautiful Britain: Abbotsford. London: Adam and Charles Black, 1912.

Davis, Martin. *Mary Marchioness of Downshire and Baroness Sandys, 1764–1836*. Worcester: Ombersley Archive Publication, 2020.

Dawson, Deidre and Pierre Morère. *Scotland and France in the Enlightenment*. Lewisburg, PA: Bucknell University Press, 2004.

Diaz, Delphine and Sylvie Aprile. *Banished: Traveling the Roads of Exile in Nineteenth-Century Europe*. Berlin: De Gruyter, 2022.

Duncan, Ian. *Scott's Shadow: The Novel in Romantic Edinburgh*. Princeton, NJ: Princeton University Press, 2007.

Duplessis, Charles. *L'équitation en France: ses écoles et ses maitres, depuis le XVe siècle à nos jours*. Paris: Berger-Levrault et compagnie, 1892.

Edgeworth, Richard Lovell and Maria Edgeworth. *Memoirs of Richard Lovell Edgeworth, Esq, Begun by Himself and Concluded by His Daughter Maria Edgeworth*. Vol. 1. London: Hunter, 1820. https://archive.org/details/memoirsofrichard00edge.

Ezell, Margaret J. M. *Social Authorship and the Advent of Print*. Baltimore, MD: Johns Hopkins University Press, 1999.

Foster, Joseph. *Almuni Oronienses: The Members of the University of Oxford, 1715–1886*. Oxford: James Parker and Company, 1888. www.google.fr/books/edition/Alumni_Oxonienses/Av8wAQAAMAAJ?hl=en&gbpv=0.

Gerbod, Paul. *Les Voyageurs français à la découverte des îles britanniques du 18e siècle à nos jours*. Paris: L'Harmattan, 1995.

Gilbert, Sandra and Susan Gubar. *The Madwoman in the Attic: The Woman Writer and the Nineteenth-Century Literary Imagination*. New Haven, CT: Yale University Press, 2000.

Graham, Lesley. *The Production and Dissemination of Knowledge in Scotland: La production et la diffusion des savoirs en Écosse*. Besançon: Presses Universitaires de Franche-Comté, 2017.

Grosclaude, Pierre. *La Vie Intellectuelle à Lyon dans la seconde moitié du 18e siècle*. Paris: Éditions Auguste Picard, 1933.

Gury, Jacques. *Le Voyage outre-Manche: Anthologie de voyageurs français de Voltaire à Mac Orlan du 18e au 20e siècle*. Paris: Robert Laffont, 1999.

Gwynn, Robin. *Huguenot Heritage. The History and Contribution of the Huguenots in Britain*. London: Routledge and Kegan Paul, 1985.

Hare, Augustus J. C. *The Life and Letters of Maria Edgeworth*. Vol. 2. Gutenberg, 2005. www.gutenberg.org/cache/epub/9095/pg9095.html.

Heber, Richard and R. H. Cholmondeley. *The Heber Letters, 1783–1832*. Batchworth Press, 1950.

Irving, Washington. 'Abbotsford'. *Crayon Miscellany*. New York: George P. Putnam, 1835.

Jansen, Jan C. and Kirsten McKenzie. *Mobility and Coercion in an Age of Wars and Revolution: A Global History, c. 1750–1830*. Cambridge: Cambridge University Press, 2024.

Kassler, Jamie Croy. *The Science of Music in Britain, 1714–1830: A Catalogue of Writings, Lectures, and Inventions*. New York: Garland, 1979.

Kelly, Debra and Martyn Cornick. *A History of the French in London: Liberty, Equality, Opportunity*. Institute of Historical Research Conference Series. London: University of London Press, 2013. www.jstor.org/stable/j.ctv512xmz.

Lok, Matthijs. *Europe against Revolution: Conservatism, Enlightenment, and the Making of the Past*. Oxford: Oxford University Press, 2023.

Maigron, Louis. *Le Roman historique à l'époque romantique: Essai sur l'influence de Walter Scott*. Paris: Champion, 1912.

Marsh-Caldwell, Anne. *The Protestant Reformation in France; Or, History of the Huguenots*. Vol. 1. London: Richard Bentley, 1847. https://books.google.fr/books?id=gj_HACDtD3UC.

Mason, Shena *The Hardware Man's Daughter: Matthew Boulton and His 'Dear Girl'*. Chichester: Phillimore, 2005.

Maxwell, Richard. *The Historical Novel in Europe, 1650–1950*. Cambridge: Cambridge University Press, 2009.

McCall, Hugh. *The House of Downshire*, 2nd ed. Belfast: Mullan, 1881.

Middelhoff, Frederike, Jennifer Leetsch, and Miriam Wallraven. *Configurations of Migration: Knowledges, Imaginaries, Media*. Boston, MA: De Gruyter, 2023.

Monnickendam, Andrew. *The Novels of Walter Scott and His Literary Relations, Mary Brunton, Susan Ferrier and Christian Johnstone*. Basingstoke: Palgrave Macmillan, 2013.

Moores, John Richard. *Representations of France in English Satirical Prints, 1740–1832*. Basingstoke: Palgrave Macmillan, 2015.

Murphy, Andrew. *Ireland, Reading and Cultural Nationalism, 1790–1930: Bringing the Nation to Book*. Cambridge: Cambridge University Press, 2018.

Pestel, Friedemann, Juliette Reboul, and Matthijs Lok. *Cosmopolitan Conservatisms: Countering Revolution in Transnational Networks, Ideas and Movements (c. 1700–1930)*. Studies in the History of Political Thought 16. Leiden: Brill, 2021.

Pichot, Amédée. *Voyage historique et littéraire en Angleterre et en Écosse*. Vol. 3. Paris: Ladvocat and C. Gosselin, 1825.

Piozzi, Hester Lynch. *Observations and Reflections Made in the Course of a Journey through France, Italy, and Germany*. Vol. 1. London: A. Strahan and T. Cadell, 1789. https://gallica.bnf.fr/ark:/12148/bpt6k350076/f38.item.

Pittock, Murray. *The Reception of Sir Walter Scott in Europe*. London: Continuum, 2006.

Plassart, Anna. *Scottish Enlightenment and the French Revolution*. Cambridge: Cambridge University Press, 2011.

Polasky, Janet. *Asylum between Nations: Refugees in a Revolutionary Era*. New Haven, CT: Yale University Press, 2023. https://doi.org/10.2307/jj.1640548.

Reboul, Juliette. *French Emigration to Great Britain in Response to the French Revolution*. War, Culture and Society, 1750–1850. Basingstoke: Palgrave Macmillan, 2017.

Reboul, Juliette and Laure Philip. *French Emigrants in Revolutionised Europe: Connected Histories and Memories*. War, Culture and Society, 1750–1850. Basingstoke: Palgrave Macmillan, 2019.

Richardson, John. *The Annals of London: A Year-by-Year Record of a Thousand Years of History*. Berkeley: University of California Press, 2000.

Sabiron, Céline. *Écrire la frontière: Walter Scott ou les chemins de l'errance*. Provence: Presses Universitaires de Provence, 2016.

Saint-Aubain, Jean de. *Histoire de la ville de Lyon, ancienne et moderne, avec les figures de toutes ses vues*. Lyon: Chez Benoist Coral, en ruë Mercière à l'enseigne de la Victoire, 1666.

Schellenberg, Betty A. *Literary Coteries and the Making of Modern Print Culture, 1740–1790*. Cambridge: Cambridge University Press, 2016.

Scouloudi, Irene. *Huguenots in Britain and Their French Background, 1550–1800*. Basingstoke: Palgrave Macmillan, 1987. https://archive.org/details/huguenotsinbrita0000unse.

Showalter, Elaine. *A Literature of Their Own: British Women Novelists from Bronte to Lessing*. Princeton: Princeton University Press, 1977.

Stanwood, Owen. *The Global Refuge: Huguenots in an Age of Empire*. Oxford: Oxford University Press, 2020.

Starke, Mariana. *Travels in Italy, between 1792 and 1798; Containing a View of the Late Revolutions, with a Supplement Comprising Instructions for Travelling in France*. Vol. 2. Oxford: Oxford University Press, 1802. https://books.google.fr/books?id=ZBUIAAAAQAAJ.

Talbott, Siobhan. *Conflict, Commerce and Franco-Scottish Relations, 1560–1713*. London: Taylor and Francis, 2014.

Thomson, Ann, Simon Burrows, and Edmond Dziembowski. *Cultural Transfers: France and Britain in the Long Eighteenth Century*. Oxford: Voltaire Foundation, 2010.

Tomalin, Marcus. *The French Language and British Literature, 1756–1830*. Abingdon, Oxon: Routledge, 2016. https://doi.org/10.4324/9781315557991.

Tombs, Robert and Isabelle Tombs. *That Sweet Enemy: Britain and France, the History of a Love–Hate Relationship*. London: Vintage, 2008.

Trénard, Louis. *Histoire sociale des idées. Lyon, de l'Encyclopédie au Préromantisme*. Paris: Presses Universitaires de France, 1958.

Trim, David J.B. *The Huguenots: History and Memory in Transnational Context*. Studies in the History of Christian Traditions. Vol. 156. Leiden: Brill, 2011.

Vickery, Amanda. *The Gentleman's Daughter: Women's Lives in Georgian England*. New Haven, CT: Yale University Press, 1998.

Wazek, Norbert. *L'Écosse des lumières: Hume, Smith, Ferguson*, Paris: Presses Universitaires de France, 2003.

Book Chapters and Articles

Barnaby, Paul. '"Another Tale of *Old Mortality*": The Translations of Auguste-Jean-Baptiste Defauconpret in the French Reception of Scott'. In Murray Pittock, ed. *The Reception of Sir Walter Scott in Europe*. London: Continuum, 2006, 31–44.

Beauchamp, Peter. 'Zoffany's Executor Charles François Dumergue (1739–1814): And His Family's Dealings with Artists'. *British Art Journal* 13.1 (Spring/Summer 2012): 3–6.

Bour, Isabelle. 'John Gibson Lockhart's *Memoirs of the Life of Sir Walter Scott, Bart.*, or the Absent Author'. *Studies in Scottish Literature* 29.1 (1996): 37–44. https://scholarcommons.sc.edu/cgi/viewcontent.cgi?article=1359&context=ssl.

'Richard Lovell Edgeworth, or the Paradoxes of a "Philosophical" Life'. In *Figures de l'intellectuel en Irlande* 34.2 (2009). https://doi.org/10.40000/etudesirlandaises.1600.

Bulletin of the History of Dentistry, vol. 41 (1993).

Carpenter, Kirsty. 'Emigration in Politics and Imaginations'. In David Andress, ed.*The Oxford Handbook of the French Revolution*. Oxford: Oxford University Press, 2015, 330–345.

Carrez, Jean-Pierre. 'La Salpêtrière de Paris sous l'Ancien Régime: lieu d'exclusion et de punition pour femmes'. *Criminocorpus*. Varia, 2008. https://doi.org/10.4000/criminocorpus.264. http://journals.openedition.org/criminocorpus/264.

Coquillard, Isabelle. 'Les médecins parisiens et la diffusion du savoir médical au 18e siècle: des savants pédagogues'. In Dominique Barjot, ed. *Transmission et circulation des savoirs scientifiques et techniques*. Paris: Éditions du Comité des travaux historiques et scientifiques, 2020, 38–50.

Degueurce, Christophe. 'Claude Bourgelat and the Creation of the First Veterinary schools'. *C.R. Biologies* 335 (2012): 334–342.

Doucet, Corinne. 'Les académies équestres et l'éducation de la noblesse (XVIe–XVIIIe siècle)'. *Revue historique* 628 (2003/2004): 817–836.

Ferris, Ina. 'Scott's Authorship and Book Culture'. In Fiona Robertson, ed. *The Edinburgh Companion to Sir Walter Scott*. Edinburgh: Edinburgh University Press, 2012, 9–21.

Green, Frank C. 'Scott's French Correspondence'. *Modern Language Review* 52.1 (Jan. 1957): 35–49.

Gwynn, Robin. 'The Number of Huguenot Immigrants in England, 1680–1700'. *Journal of Historical Geography* 9.4 (1983): 384–395.

Kramer, Lloyd. 'Émigrés and Migrations during the French Revolution'. Special Forum. *Historical Reflections/Réflexions Historiques* 48. 3 (2022): 1–68.

Lyons, Martyn. 'The Audience for Romanticism: Walter Scott in France, 1815–1851'. *European History Quarterly* 14.1 (January 1984): 21–46. https://doi.org/10.1177/02656914840140010.

Marshall, Keith. 'France and the Scottish Press, 1700–1800'. *Studies in Scottish Literature* 13.1 (1978): 1–14. https://scholarcommons.sc.edu/ssl/vol13/iss1/3.

Maxwell, Richard. 'Scott in France'. In Murray Pittock, ed. *The Reception of Sir Walter Scott in Europe*. London: Continuum, 2006, 11–30.

McKinstry, Sam and Marie Fletcher. 'The Personal Account Books of Sir Walter Scott'. *Accounting Historians Journal* 29.2 (Dec. 2002): 59–89.

McLeman-Carnie, Janette. 'Sir Walter Scott and the French Press: Paris 1826.' *International Review of Scottish Studies* 25 (June 2007): 26–52.

Pellat Jean-Christophe and Nelly Andrieux-Reix. 'Histoire d'É ou de la variation des usages graphiques à la différenciation réglée'. *Langue française* 51.3 (2006): 7–24. https://doi.org/10.3917/lf.151.0007.

Pestel, Friedemann. 'The Colors of Exile in the Age of Revolutions: New Perspectives for French Émigré Studies'. *Yearbook of Transnational History* 4 (2021): 27–68.

Pestel, Friedemann. 'The Age of Emigrations: French Emigrés and Global Entanglements of Political Exile'. In *French Emigrants in Revolutionised Europe*. Ed. Reboul and Philip. Basingstoke: Palgrave Macmillan, 2019, 205–231.

Pestel, Friedemann. 'French Revolution and Migration after 1789', *European History Online (EGO)*, 7 Nov. 2017. www.ieg-ego.eu/pestelf-2017-en.

Pope-Hennessy, Una, Dame. 'Sir Walter Scott and Religion'. *The Downside Review* 50.1 (1932): 24–32. https://doi.org/10.1177/00125806305000102.

Pugh, Leslie P. 'Vial de St Bel (1750–1793)'. *British Veterinary Journal* 118 (1962): 262–267.

Rance, Karine. 'L'historiographie de l'émigration'. In Philippe Bourdin, ed. *Les noblesses françaises dans l'Europe de la Révolution*. Histoire. Rennes: Presses Universitaires de Rennes, 2010, 355–368.

Sabiron, Céline. 'Handing Over Walter Scott: The Writer's Hand on the English and French Marketplace'. In Susan Oliver, ed. *Walter Scott: New Interpretations*. Yearbook of English Studies 47. Cambridge: Modern Humanities Research Association, 2017, 58–74.

Taylor, Brian W. 'Richard Lovell Edgeworth'. *Irish Journal of Education* 20.1 (Summer 1986): 27–50.

Unpublished Theses

Dexter, Elizabeth Anthony. 'Papers of Elizabeth A. Dexter'. 1955–1962. Coll-1081. 'Archives and Manuscripts' Collections. Edinburgh University Library.

Corrected Typescript of 'Sir Walter Scott and His Wife: The Happy Marriage and the Mystery', 1960. MS.23066. National Library of Scotland.

Conference Papers

Archer-Thompson, Kirsty. '"Oh, What a Tangled Web She Weaves:" Marguerite Charlotte Charpentier, the Fair Unknown', 'Alliance, Antagonism and Authorship: Eleventh International Scott Conference', Université Paris-Sorbonne, 10–13 juil. 2018.

Shepherd, Deirdre. 'The Life of Marguerite Charlotte Charpentier: Disorderly Other' for 'The Edinburgh Sir Walter Scott Club', 7 March 2019. www.youtube.com/watch?v=2rA8DfZYiTo.

Dictionaries

Dictionary of Irish Biography. https://doi.org/10.3318/dib.004017.v1.

Oxford Dictionary of National Biography. www.oxforddnb.com.

Websites

Archives de Lyon. www.fondsenligne.archives-lyon.fr.

Archives nationales de France. www.siv.archives-nationales.culture.gouv.fr.

Millgate Union Catalogue of Walter Scott Correspondence. digital.nls.uk/catalogues/walter-scott-correspondence.

National Library of Wales. https://viewer.library.wales.

Public Records of Ireland, Belfast. https://apps.proni.gov.uk/eCatNI_IE/SearchResults.aspx.

Somerset Heritage Centre. https://discovery.nationalarchives.gov.uk.

The Walter Scott Digital Archive. www.walterscott.lib.ed.ac.uk.

Acknowledgements

I am grateful to independent researcher Reine-Marie Faure for inviting me to speak at the Lyon conference 'Le Destin romanesque de Charlotte Charpentier' on 8 March 2023 – symbolically Woman's Day – which rekindled my interest in this enigmatic figure. Special thanks to the dearly missed Abbotsford archivist Kirsty Archer-Thompson for her generous insights and guidance in the early stages of my research. This Element is dedicated to her. I also appreciate the support from archivists across the United Kingdom: Angela Schofield at the Advocates Library, Rebecca O'Neill at the Public Record of Northern Ireland, Kai Sinclair at Lancashire Archives, Helen Glenn at Birmingham Library, and especially James Hamilton and Diana Stoica at the Signet Library, Edinburgh.

My dear colleagues and friends in the 'Walter Scott' community have been indispensable. I am particularly grateful to Professor Alison Lumsden and Dr Ainsley McIntosh for their guidance on the Abbotsford collection, and to Ali for the personal tour she gave me on 16 April 2024. Special thanks to Dr Paul Barnaby at Edinburgh University Library for his support with the Dexter Papers, and to Dr Deirdre Shepherd, who first brought Dexter's unpublished thesis to my attention.

Finally, I warmly thank Professor Eve Tavor Bannet for her invaluable input throughout the writing process. I am also grateful to the University of Lorraine and the head of my Interdisciplinarités Dans les Études Anglophones research centre, Professor Nathalie Collé, along with Pôle TELL, for funding my research trips to Edinburgh (April 2024) and London (May 2024). My thanks as well to the French Society for English Studies committee for awarding a grant to cover image publication costs for this Element.

Cambridge Elements

Eighteenth-Century Connections

Series Editors
Eve Tavor Bannet
University of Oklahoma

Eve Tavor Bannet is George Lynn Cross Professor Emeritus, University of Oklahoma and editor of *Studies in Eighteenth-Century Culture*. Her monographs include *Empire of Letters: Letter Manuals and Transatlantic Correspondence 1688–1820* (Cambridge, 2005), *Transatlantic Stories and the History of Reading, 1720–1820* (Cambridge, 2011), and *Eighteenth-Century Manners of Reading: Print Culture and Popular Instruction in the Anglophone Atlantic World* (Cambridge, 2017). She is editor of *British and American Letter Manuals 1680–1810* (Pickering & Chatto, 2008), *Emma Corbett* (Broadview, 2011) and, with Susan Manning, *Transatlantic Literary Studies* (Cambridge, 2012).

Markman Ellis
Queen Mary University of London

Markman Ellis is Professor of Eighteenth-Century Studies at Queen Mary University of London. He is the author of *The Politics of Sensibility: Race, Gender and Commerce in the Sentimental Novel* (1996), *The History of Gothic Fiction* (2000), *The Coffee-House: a Cultural History* (2004), and *Empire of Tea* (co-authored, 2015). He edited *Eighteenth-Century Coffee-House Culture* (4 vols, 2006) and *Tea and the Tea-Table in Eighteenth-Century England* (4 vols 2010), and co-editor of *Discourses of Slavery and Abolition* (2004) and *Prostitution and Eighteenth-Century Culture: Sex, Commerce and Morality* (2012).

Advisory Board
Linda Bree, *Independent*
Claire Connolly, *University College Cork*
Gillian Dow, *University of Southampton*
James Harris, *University of St Andrews*
Thomas Keymer, *University of Toronto*
Jon Mee, *University of York*
Carla Mulford, *Penn State University*
Nicola Parsons, *University of Sydney*
Manushag Powell, *Purdue University*
Robbie Richardson, *University of Kent*
Shef Rogers, *University of Otago*
Eleanor Shevlin, *West Chester University*
David Taylor, *Oxford University*
Chloe Wigston Smith, *University of York*
Roxann Wheeler, *Ohio State University*
Eugenia Zuroski, *MacMaster University*

About the Series
Exploring connections between verbal and visual texts and the people, networks, cultures and places that engendered and enjoyed them during the long Eighteenth Century, this innovative series also examines the period's uses of oral, written and visual media, and experiments with the digital platform to facilitate communication of original scholarship with both colleagues and students.

Cambridge Elements

Eighteenth-Century Connections

Elements in the Series

The Domino and the Eighteenth-Century London Masquerade: A Social Biography of a Costume
Meghan Kobza

Paratext Printed with New English Plays, 1660–1700
Robert D. Hume

The Art of the Actress
Fashioning Identities

A Performance History of The Fair Penitent
Elaine McGirr

Labour of the Stitch: The Making and Remaking of Fashionable Georgian Dress
Serena Dyer

Early English Periodicals and Early Modern Social Media
Margaret J. M. Ezell

Reading with the Burneys: Patronage, Paratext, and Performance
Sophie Coulombeau

Jacobitism and Cultural Memory, 1688–1830
Leith Davis

On Wonder: Literature and Science in the Long Eighteenth Century
Tita Chico

The Epistemologies of Progress
Richard Adelman

Networks of Reception in the Eighteenth-Century British Press and Laurence Sterne
Mary Newbould

Unveiling Lady Scott: Walter Scott, French Influence and Transcultural Connections
Céline Sabiron

A full series listing is available at: www.cambridge.org/EECC

For EU product safety concerns, contact us at Calle de José Abascal, 56–1°, 28003 Madrid, Spain or eugpsr@cambridge.org.

www.ingramcontent.com/pod-product-compliance
Lightning Source LLC
LaVergne TN
LVHW011850060526
838200LV00054B/4260